Border Games

A volume in the series

Cornell Studies in Political Economy

EDITED BY PETER J. KATZENSTEIN

A full list of titles in the series appears at the end of the book

Border Games

POLICING THE
U.S.-MEXICO DIVIDE

PETER ANDREAS

CORNELL UNIVERSITY PRESS

Ithaca and London

First published 2000 by Cornell University Press

Printed in the United States of America

Library of Congress Cataloging-in-Publication Data

Andreas, Peter, 1965–
    Border games : policing the U.S.–Mexico divide / Peter Andreas.
       p.   cm. — (Cornell studies in political economy.)
    Includes bibliographical references and index.
    ISBN 0-8014-3796-2 (cloth)
    1. Smuggling—Mexican-American Border Region.   2. Drug traffic—
Government policy—United States.   3. Illegal aliens—Government policy—
United States.   4. Border patrols—Mexican-American Border Region.   5. Mexican-
American Border Region—Economic conditions.   6. United States—Boundaries—
Mexico.   7. Mexico—Boundaries—United States.   8. Boundaries.   I. Title.
II. Series.

   HJ6690+

                                          00-024022

Cornell University Press strives to use environmentally responsible suppliers and materials to the fullest extent possible in the publishing of its books. Such materials include vegetable-based, low-VOC inks and acid-free papers that are recycled, totally chlorine-free, or partly composed of nonwood fibers. Books that bear the logo of the FSC (Forest Stewardship Council) use paper taken from forests that have been inspected and certified as meeting the highest standards for environmental and social responsibility. For further information, visit our website at www.cornellpress.cornell.edu.

Cloth printing   10 9 8 7 6 5 4 3 2 1

2/00

Contents

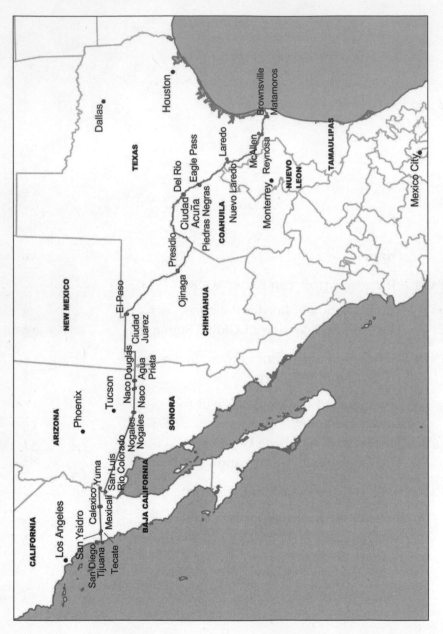

The U.S.-Mexico border

Preface

Standing inside the front entrance of the public affairs office at the Border Patrol's sector headquarters south of San Diego not long ago, I immediately noticed two large photographs prominently displayed on the wall. They show the same stretch of the California-Mexico border, historically the single most popular crossing point for illegal migrants heading north. The first photograph, taken in the early 1990s, shows a mangled chain-link fence and crowds of people milling about, seemingly oblivious that the border even exists. The Border Patrol is nowhere in sight. The image is of a chaotic border that is defied, defeated, and undefended. The second photograph, taken a number of years later, shows a sturdy ten-foot-high metal wall backed up by lightposts and Border Patrol all-terrain vehicles alertly monitoring the line; no people gather on either side. The image is of a quiet and orderly border that deters and defends against illegal crossings. The new wall was built by U.S. Army reservists out of 180,000 metal sheets originally made for temporary landing fields during military operations. Mexicans have dubbed it the "Iron Curtain."

These sharply contrasting pictures are part of a larger transformation in the policing of the nearly 2,000-mile-long U.S.-Mexico boundary. In a relatively short period of time, border control has changed from a low-intensity, low-maintenance, and politically marginal activity to a high-intensity, high-maintenance campaign commanding enormous political attention on both sides of the territorial divide. Reflecting the new enthusiasm, the size of the U.S. Border Patrol has more than doubled since 1993. An advertising agency has even coined a catchy slogan to woo thousands of new recruits: "A career with borders but no boundaries." The border enforcement role of many other federal agencies has also expanded at a

People mingle around broken-down border fence, about one mile west of the San Ysidro port of entry, San Diego–Tijuana border, 1991. (Photo courtesy of the U.S. Border Patrol.)

New fence, about one mile west of the San Ysidro port of entry, San Diego–Tijuana border, 1999. (Photo courtesy of the U.S. Border Patrol.)

rapid pace. The buildup, moreover, is not restricted to the U.S. side of the line. The Mexican military, for example, has been placed in charge of the antidrug effort in many of the country's northern states.

What explains the sharp escalation of border policing? That is the underlying question of this book. It is particularly intriguing because the tightening of border controls has happened at a time and place otherwise defined by the relaxation of state controls and the *opening* of the border—most notably through the North American Free Trade Agreement (NAFTA). Noticeably left out of NAFTA are two of Mexico's most important exports: illegal drugs and migrant labor. Instead, tariffs on these smuggled goods (or "bads," depending on one's perspective) are rising in the form of more intensive policing. The result has been the construction of both a borderless economy and a barricaded border. The politics of opening the border to legal economic flows is closely connected to the politics of making it appear more closed to illegal flows. I argue that the escalation of border policing has ultimately been less about deterring the flow of drugs and migrants than about recrafting the image of the border and symbolically reaffirming the state's territorial authority. Those who view border enforcement as either puny and ineffective or draconian and inhumane too often fail to appreciate its perceptual and symbolic dimensions.

Indeed, border policing has some of the features of a ritualized spectator sport, but in this case the objective of the game is to tame rather than inflame the passions of the spectators. Calling it a "game" is meant not to belittle or trivialize border policing and its consequences but rather to capture its performative and audience-directed nature. The game metaphor also draws attention to the strategic interaction between border enforcers and illegal border crossers. It provides a healthy antidote to the metaphors of war and natural disaster—such as "invasion" and "flood"—more commonly used to characterize the problems of immigration and drug control.

The U.S.-Mexico boundary is the busiest land border in the world, the longest and most dramatic meeting point between a rich and a poor country, and the site of the most intensive interaction between law enforcement and law evasion. Nowhere else has the state been so aggressively loosening and tightening its territorial grip at the same time. Nowhere else do the contrasting state practices of market liberalization and criminalization more visibly overlap. It was these provocative features that initially captured my attention. A comparative perspective, however, suggests that while the U.S.-Mexico border is unusual, it is by no means unique. Other meeting places between rich and poor countries, most obviously the eastern and southern external borders of the European Union, show similar dynamics. Framing the study more broadly reveals that within a general escalation of law enforcement, different forms and trajectories of escalation reflect distinct historical legacies and regional political and institutional contexts.

In writing about border policing I have crossed disciplinary borders. Although written in the field of international politics, the book borrows from and speaks to a more diverse audience, including political economists, criminologists and sociologists of law, anthropologists, geographers, historians, and specialists in public policy and area studies. At the same time, that audience extends outside of academia to the policy community. Having lived in both the policy world and the academic world, I am well aware of the borders that divide the two—and I continue to try to bridge them.

In carrying out my research I relied on a wide range of primary and secondary source materials, including many government documents and media reports. An important part of the research involved interviews with state officials, journalists, policy analysts, and representatives of non-governmental organizations in the United States, Mexico, and Western Europe. I consulted U.S. officials from the Customs Service, the Drug Enforcement Administration, the Federal Bureau of Investigation, the National Security Council, the Immigration and Naturalization Service and (its uniformed enforcement wing) the Border Patrol, the Department of Defense, the Office of the U.S. Attorney for the Southern District of California, the State Department's Bureau of International Narcotics Matters and Law Enforcement Affairs, the White House Office of National Drug Control Policy, and the Narcotics Affairs Section of the U.S. Embassy in Mexico City. Mexican officials interviewed included representatives from the Office of the Attorney General, the Secretariat for External Relations, the Secretariat for Governmental Affairs, the Mexican Embassy in Washington, and the Mexican Consulate in San Diego. In Europe I talked with officials from the German Federal Border Police, the German Customs Service, the German Federal Investigative Police, the Spanish Ministry of the Interior, the Ceuta (Spain) Police Department, the European Commission in Brussels, and the United Nations Drug Control Program in Vienna.

A few words of caution are called for regarding research in this particular area. First, much of law enforcement is by nature secretive, and the official documents produced for public consumption can conceal as much as they reveal. They are nevertheless enormously useful for my purposes, because an essential part of the story is showing how the policing face of the state presents itself in public. Second, it is obviously impossible to calculate with any precision the size and scope of illegal cross-border flows; the published government statistics on drug trafficking and illegal immigration necessarily represent rough estimates. Readers are advised to keep these limitations in mind. Indeed, the packaging of official data is very much part of the political process of image crafting which can help to promote support for more policing.

Numerous people helped me travel down the path of turning an idea into a book. Most important, Peter Katzenstein's intellectual wisdom and generosity were crucial at every stage. Theodore Lowi and Hector Schamis provided additional encouragement and advice. James Kurth and Ken Sharpe, who nurtured my early interest in the study of politics, have continued to be sources of inspiration and support. Many friends and colleagues made the project feel like a team effort, and I especially thank Amy Gurowitz and Jim Ron for their dependable long-distance camaraderie. Earlier collaborative work with Ken Sharpe, Eva Bertram, and Morris Blachman advanced my understanding of the politics of drug control.

For valuable discussions and suggestions, I thank Rawi Abdelal, Walter Actis, Malcolm Anderson, Sigrid Arzst, John Bailey, Carol Bergman, Jack Blum, Lothar Brock, Kitty Calavita, Dana Calvo, Carlos Celaya, Jorge Chabat, Bill Chambliss, Wayne Cornelius, Peter Cullen, Paolo De Mas, Herbert Dittgen, Tim Dunn, Graham Farrell, Marty Finnemore, Gary Freeman, Rich Friman, Albrecht Funk, Tim Golden, Guadalupe González, Joseph Gusfield, C. R. Hibbs, Juliet Johnson, Elizabeth Joyce, Gabriela Lemus, Enrico Marcelli, Roberto Martinez, Gary Marx, Bill McDonald, Philip Muus, Ethan Nadelmann, Jesús Núñez Villaverde, Demetrios Papademetriou, Ana Planet, James Rosenau, Marc Rosenblum, Sebastian Rotella, Cathy Schneider, Louise Shelley, James Sheptyki, Peter Skerry, Peter Smith, Rob Smith, David Spener, Paul Stares, Marcelo Suárez-Orozco, Celia Toro, John Torpey, John Walsh, Phil Williams, Carol Wise, and Carolyn Wong. I am especially thankful to those who read draft chapters: Carol Andreas, Joel Andreas, Michael Barnett, Katrina Burgess, Amy Gurowitz, Peter Katzenstein, Jonathan Kirshner, James Kurth, Theodore Lowi, Joe Nevins, Jim Ron, Hector Schamis, Tim Snyder, Ken Sharpe, and Van Whiting. Roger Haydon at Cornell University Press expertly guided the manuscript through review and revision. Pat Sterling handled the copyediting with great attention and care.

I am deeply indebted to the many people on both sides of the U.S.-Mexico border and across the Atlantic who took time from their busy schedules for long interviews. For helping me gain access to the federal law enforcement agencies along the border, special appreciation goes to Alan Bersin and his staff at the Office of the U.S. Attorney for the Southern District of California.

A year at the Brookings Institution proved ideal for conducting research and opening doors in Washington, D.C. I particularly thank the Foreign Policy Studies Program and the library staff at Brookings for helping me make the most of my stay. I owe much to those in Washington who provided access to specialized research materials: Raphael Perl at the Congressional Research Service, Kate Doyle at the National Security Archive, Mort Goren at the Drug Enforcement Administration library, and Marian Smith at the Immigration and Naturalization Service library.

As a base for both research and writing near the border, I could not have asked for a better place than the Center for U.S.-Mexican Studies of the University of California at San Diego. I thank the staff and my colleagues there, as well as those at the neighboring Center for Iberian and Latin American Studies, for their encouragement and support. This book was completed during my fellowship at the Harvard Academy for International and Area Studies, Weatherhead Center for International Affairs. Many people helped to make my time at Harvard both productive and enjoyable. I especially thank Samuel Huntington and Jorge Domínguez for providing the institutional support for a two-day conference on North American and European border controls. I also express my appreciation to Reed College for making it possible for me to postpone my arrival in Portland while I finished the writing and my fellowship appointment.

Parts of this book draw from my earlier work: "U.S.-Mexico: Open Markets, Closed Border," *Foreign Policy* 103 (summer 1996): 51–70; "The U.S. Immigration Control Offensive: Constructing an Image of Order on the Southwest Border," in *Crossings: Mexican Immigration in Interdisciplinary Perspective* (Cambridge: Harvard University Press, 1998); "The Escalation of U.S. Immigration Control in the Post-NAFTA Era," reprinted by permission of *Political Science Quarterly* 113, no. 4 (1998–99): 591–615; and "Smuggling Wars: Law Enforcement and Law Evasion in a Changing World," in *Transnational Crime in the Americas,* ed. Tom Farer (New York: Routledge, 1999). Portions of my research were presented at workshops, conferences, and seminars sponsored by the Social Science Research Council–MacArthur Foundation, the Council on Foreign Relations, the Inter-American Dialogue, the Brookings Institution, the American Political Science Association, the International Studies Association, the Latin American Studies Association, the Law and Society Association, the New England Council on Latin American Studies, Brown University, Cornell University, Harvard University, Syracuse University, Tufts University, the University of California at San Diego, the University of Pittsburgh, and the University of Washington. My thanks go to those who listened and offered constructive feedback.

Generous financial support for this work came from grants by the SSRC–MacArthur Foundation Program on International Peace and Security, the Brookings Institution, the Mellon Foundation, the Institute for the Study of World Politics, and the Harvard Academy for International and Area Studies. Funding for research travel was provided by Cornell University's Peace Studies Program, the International Political Economy Program, the Einaudi Center for International Studies, and the Department of Government.

Finally, my very personal thanks go to my parents, who provided much-appreciated moral support, and to my wife, Jasmina, who always reminded me of the more important things in life. To them I dedicate this book.

PETER ANDREAS

Cambridge, Massachusetts

Part I

Introduction and Background

CHAPTER ONE

The Escalation of Border Policing

All states claim the sovereign right to control their borders, but the focus of their concern has varied over time. In the post–Cold War era of economic integration, many states are less worried about deterring militaries or imposing tariffs on commerce than about keeping out "undesirables." Leading the list of perceived threats are the smuggling of migrants and mind-altering substances (particularly cocaine, heroin, and marijuana). The tightening of controls over these cross-border flows is the most notable exception to the liberalization of the world economy. Here the advice of otherwise influential free-market proponents has fallen on deaf ears.[1]

Clandestine cross-border activities such as illegal migration and drug trafficking are not new, of course. After all, border law evasion is as old as border law enforcement. What is new is that policing these border crossings has been elevated from the status of "low politics" to "high politics," involving a shift in the definition of security threats and in the practice of security policy. Crime fighting, not war fighting, increasingly defines the border priorities of many states. This transformation has been most pronounced along the geographic fault lines that divide rich and poor countries, particularly the southern border of the United States and the eastern and southern external borders of the European Union (EU).

This book traces the practice and politics of policing the flow of drugs and immigrants across the U.S.-Mexico border. I offer an explanation of why such policing has sharply escalated in recent years, placing causal im-

1. Milton Friedman and the *Economist* advocate drug legalization, and the *Wall Street Journal* promotes open borders for labor.

portance on the often unintended feedback effects of past policy choices, the political and bureaucratic incentives and rewards for key state actors, and the symbolic and perceptual appeal of escalation regardless of its actual deterrent effect. For analytical leverage, I also extend the analysis to the southern border of Spain and the eastern border of Germany, where the buildup of policing is part of an ambitious new collaborative effort to harden the outer perimeter of the European Union. Trends across these EU borders parallel but also significantly depart from the trends across the U.S.-Mexico border.

On both sides of the U.S.-Mexico borderline, escalation has translated into tougher laws, rising budgets and agency growth,[2] the deployment of more sophisticated equipment and surveillance technologies, and a growing fusion between law enforcement and national security institutions and missions. Of course, the most visible—and certainly most symbolic—sign of escalation has been the construction of more and bigger physical barriers. Escalation is also evident more generally in the sharper tone of the policy discourse about the border and the heightened prominence of "law and order" issues on both U.S. and Mexican policy agendas. The border-policing offensive is reflected in high-profile U.S. enforcement initiatives during the past decade, such as Operation Gatekeeper, Operation Hold-the-Line, and Operation Hard Line. As their names suggest, these deterrence efforts have been in stark contrast to the celebratory discourse of North American integration. In other words, even as economic trends have pushed to remake the border into a bridge to facilitate rising legal flows, policing trends have reinforced the border as a barrier against illegal flows.[3]

These developments defy the conventional wisdom that borders have become increasingly irrelevant in the so-called age of globalization. Too often, territorial controls are impatiently dismissed as relics of the past.

2. The federal government spent less than $70 million in 1971 on Southwest border law enforcement. In 1997 spending on drug control alone along the same border had reached $1.7 billion. On September 16, 1998, retired General Barry R. McCaffrey, the Clinton-appointed "drug czar," testified before the Senate Foreign Relations Committee and the Senate Caucus on International Narcotics Control that there were 12,000 federal law enforcement personnel on the border, whereas "in 1987, it was a fraction of that, so there is a huge, sensible, aggressive effort to protect the American people."

3. In 1998, 278 million people, 86 million cars, and 4 million trucks and railcars legally entered the United States from Mexico. That same year, the White House estimates, more than half the cocaine and a large percentage of the heroin, marijuana, and methamphetamines consumed in the United States entered across the border from Mexico. The Immigration and Naturalization Service (INS) has calculated that 2.7 million of the estimated 5 million illegal immigrants residing permanently in the United States in 1997 came from Mexico. Office of National Drug Control Policy, *National Drug Control Strategy* (Washington, D.C.: GPO, 1999), 69; *Washington Post,* 8 February 1997.

Richard Rosecrance, for example, has optimistically proclaimed that "territory is passé," and Kenichi Ohmae has enthusiastically announced the emergence of a "borderless world."[4] A particularly fashionable view is that greater economic interdependence generates more harmonious cross-border relations and less state intervention. Glossed over is the fact that the clandestine side of cross-border economic exchange (that is, smuggling) has become a source of rising anxiety, often leading to heightened tensions and more state intervention in the form of policing. Thus, far from being dismantled and retired, the border regulatory apparatus of the state in many places is being retooled and redeployed.

While writing much in recent years about the retreat of the state and the opening of borders, scholars have been much slower to recognize the reassertion of state policing and the tightening of border controls. Especially in the field of international relations, the policing side of state border practices and the clandestine side of cross-border economic activity have long been marginalized subjects. The relative neglect of policing is puzzling, given that the lawmaking and law-enforcing authority of the state is the "bedrock of sovereignty."[5] As a core component of the state's monopoly over the legitimate means of coercion, police practices epitomize sovereignty in action. The study of policing is primarily carried out in the specialized fields of criminology and criminal justice studies, which have traditionally focused almost exclusively on domestic issues such as local crime control.[6] Far less attention has been given to the dynamics of policing on and across national borders.[7]

FORMS OF ESCALATION ACROSS THE U.S.-MEXICO BORDER

Escalation has taken very different forms in the cases of immigration and drug control. The playing field and the rules of the game are distinct in each case. Not surprisingly, the United States and Mexico define unauthorized Mexican migration in fundamentally different ways: on the U.S.

4. Richard Rosecrance, "The Rise of the Virtual State," *Foreign Affairs* 75, no. 4 (1996): 45–62; Kenichi Ohmae, *The Borderless World: Power and Strategy in an Interlinked Economy* (New York: Harper Business, 1990).

5. Janice Thomson, "State Sovereignty in International Relations: Bridging the Gap between Theory and Empirical Research," *International Studies Quarterly* 39, no. 2 (1995): 213.

6. But see William F. McDonald, "The Globalization of Criminology: The Next Frontier Is the Frontier," *Transnational Organized Crime* 1, no. 1 (1995): 1–22.

7. Exceptions include Ethan Nadelmann, *Cops across Borders: The Internationalization of U.S. Criminal Law Enforcement* (University Park: Pennsylvania State University Press, 1993); Malcolm Anderson et al., *Policing the European Union* (New York: Oxford University Press, 1996); Timothy Dunn, *The Militarization of the U.S.-Mexico Border, 1978–1992* (Austin: Center for Mexican-American Studies, University of Texas, 1996).

side it is primarily treated as a law enforcement matter; on the Mexican, as a social and economic matter.[8] Consequently, the escalation of immigration control has been largely restricted to the U.S. side of the border (though Mexico has intensified its efforts to curb the smuggling of non-Mexican nationals through Mexican territory). Drugs, on the other hand, are criminalized by both countries, and thus control efforts have been officially promoted as collaborative (even though there has been much finger pointing in both directions): the United States has been able to exert far more pressure on Mexico to curb drug smuggling than to control migrant smuggling and has extended the reach of U.S. drug enforcement personnel into Mexico (a sensitive and controversial topic in the bilateral relationship). Cross-border military and law enforcement ties are dominated by drug control concerns.

Yet despite the differences between immigration and drug control, there are core similarities. In both cases the primary target is the supply (illegal drugs, migrants, and those who smuggle them) and only secondarily the demand (consumers of drugs and employers of migrant labor); the foreign supply is defined as the main source of the problem; and deterring the supply through enhanced policing is promoted as the favored solution. How the supply is actually targeted, however, is certainly different in each case. Drugs are confiscated and destroyed; most migrants are simply sent back across the borderline to try again. Thus, although the border-crossing experience involves many risks for migrants (including abuse by smugglers and authorities), the penalties for attempting unauthorized entry have remained relatively low. Consequently, though drugs may be far more difficult to detect than migrants, the migration flow is no easier to deter.

Efforts to reduce the supply have also been much more narrowly targeted in the case of immigration control, which has overwhelmingly concentrated on the border. Enforcement at the workplace, for example, has remained noticeably lax. Drug control, in contrast, has extended from the point of production to the point of entry at the border to the point of domestic distribution and sales; indeed, it has profoundly shaped the criminal justice systems in both countries. Thus, the immigration control strategy could be described as "thin" policing, largely restricted to the border zone; drug control strategy as "thick" policing, extending to both sides of the borderline. It is along the border, however, where many of the key

8. Obviously, Mexican migration to the United States becomes illegal only once the border has been crossed without authorization (in INS terminology, EWI—"entry without inspection"). A small percentage of unauthorized border crossers were illegally in Mexico as well: i.e., non-Mexican nationals (in INS terminology, OTMs—"other than Mexicans") using Mexico as a transit point.

Mexican drug-smuggling organizations are based, that considerable U.S. and Mexican federal enforcement resources and attention are focused.

ESCALATION AS A RESPONSE TO LOSS OF STATE CONTROL?

Persistent and widespread illegal border crossings, ranging from self-smuggling by individual migrants to highly organized drug-smuggling operations by transnational criminal networks, are widely viewed as extreme examples of loss of state control over national borders. Indeed, for many scholars, journalists, and policy practitioners, "loss of control" is the dominant border narrative.[9] The basic story line is that border defenses are under siege or entirely bypassed by clandestine transnational actors.[10] Although the focus is on lack of state control rather than the increase in control efforts, embedded in the story is an implicit explanation for the escalation of force: increased policing can simply be understood as a natural policy response to an increase in illegal cross-border flows and a corresponding increase in public pressure on the state to secure its borders. In other words, the state is viewed as simply reactive, responding to a growing clandestine transnational challenge and to rising domestic pressure to meet the challenge.

The loss-of-control theme provides a powerful narrative. For law enforcement advocates, its seductively simple justification for escalation can be used to provoke alarm and mobilize support for further escalation. Alternatively, for critics it can be used to demonstrate the severe limits and even futility of such escalation. For both, however, it can lead to a fundamental misunderstanding of the nature of border policing and border smuggling. The stress on loss of control understates the degree to which the state has actually structured, conditioned, and even enabled (often unintentionally) clandestine border crossings, and overstates the degree to which the state has been able to control its borders in the past. By characterizing state policing as largely reactive, it obscures the ways in which the state itself has helped to create the very conditions that generate calls for more policing. Most important, evaluating policing practices narrowly

9. See, e.g., Susan Strange, *The Retreat of the State: The Diffusion of Power in the World Economy* (New York: Cambridge University Press, 1996); Claire Sterling, *Crime without Frontiers* (London: Warner, 1995); John Kerry, *The New War: The Web of Crime that Threatens American Security* (New York: Simon & Schuster, 1997).

10. Myron Weiner, *The Global Migration Crisis* (New York: HarperCollins, 1995), 9, echoes the popular perception that "advanced industrial countries can protect their borders from invading armies but not from hordes of individuals who slip into harbors, crawl under barbed-wire fences, and wade across rivers."

in terms of whether they attain control fails to capture their larger political and symbolic function. Border policing is not simply a policy instrument for deterring illegal crossings but a symbolic representation of state authority; it communicates the state's commitment to marking and maintaining the borderline.

The U.S.-Mexico border would seem to be the quintessential case of law enforcement escalation as a response to loss of state control. After all, that border, the most important entry to the world's largest market for illegal drugs and foreign labor, is notoriously porous. Thus, it might seem entirely predictable that the federal government would devote more attention and resources to policing it. This conventional explanation, however, obscures more than it reveals. The popular political call to "regain control" masks the fact that there actually never was a time when the border was effectively controlled. In one form or another, illegal crossings have been a defining feature of the border ever since it was established. Yet with rare exceptions, such crossings commanded limited national political attention and remained minimally policed until relatively recent times.

What has propelled the recent escalation of border policing? The loss-of-control narrative focuses attention on shifts in smuggling patterns, especially the growing power and wealth of Mexican drug-trafficking groups and the development of more daring and well-organized migrant-smuggling efforts. Yet law enforcement has not merely responded to these shifts but helped induce them. Characterizing the state as simply reacting to a growing border problem fails to capture this dynamic. Even while failing to control illegal border crossings, law enforcement has shaped their location, routes, methods, and organization. This has had enormous consequences in terms of the incentives and rewards for key actors (lawmakers, law enforcers, and law evaders) as well as for public and media perception.

The focus on loss of control also directs attention to domestic public pressure on the state to secure the border more forcefully. Lawmakers and law enforcers are certainly sensitive to public opinion; indeed, many of their actions are geared toward projecting a favorable public impression. Yet rather than simply being held captive by public opinion, political actors also compete and collaborate in crafting it. Political actors do not merely respond to public pressure to "do something" about drugs and illegal immigrants. Instead, they skillfully use images, symbols, and language to communicate what the problem is, where it comes from, and what the state is or should be doing about it. For example, the overwhelming political focus on curbing the influx of drugs and immigrants has drawn attention away from the more complex and politically divisive challenge of dealing with the enormous domestic demand for both psychoactive drugs and cheap migrant labor.

Public perception is powerfully shaped by the images of the border which politicians, law enforcement agencies, and the media project. Alarming images of a border out of control can fuel public anxiety; reassuring images of a border under control can reduce such anxiety. Depending on where along the border one chooses to look, both images are readily available. Thus, one can argue, as I do in this book, that "successful" border management depends on successful image management, and that this does not necessarily correspond with levels of actual deterrence. From this perspective, the escalation of border policing has been less about deterring than about image crafting.

THE LOGIC OF ESCALATION

Viewing the escalation of border policing as simply a response to loss of control neglects its deeper political roots and symbolic functions. Border enforcement has never been a particularly effective or efficient deterrent against drugs and illegal immigrants. Yet policing methods that are suboptimal from the perspective of a means-ends calculus of deterrence can be optimal from the political perspective of constructing an image of state authority and communicating moral resolve. In the case of the U.S.-Mexico border, signaling a commitment to the idea of deterrence and projecting an image of progress toward that goal has been more politically consequential for state actors than actually achieving deterrence.

My account of the escalation of border policing places the state front and center.[11] Escalation has been propelled by perverse and often unintended policy feedback effects and by the primacy of images and symbols for state actors engaged in border management.[12] Unraveling the logic of escalation requires taking into account how state practices shape and interact with illegal border crossings and, at the same time, project images and messages to various audiences concerned about such crossings. These images and messages are part of a public performance for which the border functions as a kind of political stage. For those state actors charged with the task of managing the border, the way their actions shape the perceptions of the audience (Congress, the media, foreign observers, the broader public) ultimately matters more than whether or not the illegal

11. This does not mean conceptualizing the state as a unitary rational actor pursuing the "national interest." Rather, multiple contradictions and interests within the state apparatus reflect different sets of relationships inside the state, between the state and society, and between the state and the international environment.

12. Paul Pierson, "When Effect Becomes Cause: Policy Feedback and Political Change," *World Politics* 45 (July 1993): 595–628.

border crossers are actually deterred. In fact, the feedback effects from some of the most popular parts of the law enforcement performance can actually create a more formidable control problem.

My emphasis on the audience-directed nature of border enforcement draws from sociological insights about the role of images and symbols in public interaction. In the social drama depicted by Erving Goffman, actors are constantly preoccupied with "engineering a convincing impression" that moral and other standards are being realized. Although the actors occupy social roles to which normative expectations are attached, they can be creative and entrepreneurial occupiers of those roles: they can comply with but also manipulate their normative environment. Similarly, in my account of the border as a political stage, state actors continuously engage in "face work" and the "art of impression management."[13] What makes the border a particularly challenging stage is that the actors are involved in a double performance, having to assure some of the audience that the border is being opened (to legal flows) while reassuring the rest of the audience that the border is being sufficiently closed (to illegal flows).

The composition of the audience varies in the cases of drug and immigration control. For Mexico's antidrug campaign the most important audience is external—Washington, D.C., especially congressional critics—whereas the U.S. drug control performance attempts primarily to impress a domestic audience, including many of the same congressional voices that worry Mexico. Leaders in both countries go to great lengths to project an image of collaboration and cooperation in fighting drugs—an image that has been tarnished by many public embarrassments but is nevertheless sustained with great care in order not to jeopardize their mutual interest in a stable and close economic relationship. They are, in a sense, on the same stage and share the goal of convincing the audience that the border is being secured. It has become an increasingly difficult performance to pull off, with a restless and sometimes even hostile audience demanding a bigger and better performance. Not wanting to ruin the show, U.S. and Mexican officials have so far opted for further escalation. An image of law enforcement teamwork across the border is noticeably missing in the case of immigration control, however; the Mexican government sends strong messages to assure its own domestic audience that it opposes the buildup

13. On the "dramaturgical" perspective in sociological theory, much of it inspired by the writings of Erving Goffman, see Dennis Brissett and Charles Edgley, eds., *Life as Theater: A Dramaturgical Sourcebook* (New York: Aldine de Gruyter, 1990). Goffman's best-known work is *The Presentation of Self in Everyday Life* (New York: Anchor, 1959), quotations from 251. Important applications of Goffman's insights to the study of international politics include Michael N. Barnett, *Dialogues in Arab Politics* (New York: Columbia University Press, 1998); and Robert Jervis, *The Logic of Images in International Relations* (New York: Columbia University Press, 1970).

of U.S. border controls. In this case, the law enforcement stage does not extend across to the Mexican side of the border.

The popularity of the border as a political stage is based as much on the *expressive role* of law enforcement (reaffirming moral boundaries) as it is on the *instrumental goal* of law enforcement (effective defense of physical boundaries). High-profile law enforcement campaigns that fail in their instrumental purpose can nevertheless be highly successful in their expressive function. Border control efforts are not only *actions* (a means to a stated instrumental end) but also *gestures* that communicate meaning.[14] Even as the enforcement performance has failed to deter illegal border crossings significantly, it has nevertheless succeeded in reaffirming the importance of the border. Indeed, failing law enforcement agencies have expanded and grown partly because of the symbolic power they derive from their position as border maintainers.[15] The seizure of drugs and arrest of smugglers take the form of a ritualistic performance, with the responsible officials keenly aware of the wider audience. Even though the drugs confiscated constitute only a fraction of the overall quantity crossing the border, and the smugglers arrested are easily replaced, these policing practices are politically popular expressions of the state's moral resolve.[16]

Border policing, from this perspective, is not only the coercive hand of the state but a ceremonial practice, not only a means to an end but an end in itself. Indeed, those who question the value of the policing effort on instrumental grounds risk being labeled defeatists whose loyalty is questioned. Fearful of the reputational costs of appearing lax on border controls, many political actors become trapped in the escalating symbolic performance. And once invested in the performance, they find it difficult to change course because of the political embarrassment of seeming to backtrack on previous commitments.[17]

The border has only recently taken center stage, however. Border policing and border smuggling were traditionally outside the national political spotlight; the audience was historically small and had minimal expec-

14. On the symbolic role of laws and their enforcement, see David Garland, "Punishment and Culture: The Symbolic Dimension of Criminal Justice," *Studies in Law, Politics, and Society* 11 (1991): 191–222; Joseph Gusfield, *Symbolic Crusade: Status Politics and the American Temperance Movement,* 2d ed. (Urbana: University of Illinois Press, 1986).

15. Law enforcement agencies are in many ways examples of the organizations referred to in the title of Marshall W. Meyer and Lynne G. Zucker's *Permanently Failing Organizations* (Newbury Park, Calif.: Sage, 1989): those that persist and may even expand despite low results.

16. As one criminologist suggests, "Drug police, like priests, are more important for what they symbolize and stand for than for what they do": Peter K. Manning, *The Narc's Game* (Cambridge, Mass.: MIT Press, 1980), 253.

17. Joel Brockner and Jeffrey Rubin, *Entrapment in Escalating Conflicts: A Social Psychological Analysis* (New York: Springer-Verlag, 1985).

tations of an impressive law enforcement performance. How and why did this change? I argue that the feedback effects of state practices on both sides of the border helped to create the very problems for which increased law enforcement has been promoted as the solution. The power-ful image effect and symbolic appeal of enhanced policing has brought with it substantial bureaucratic and political rewards—despite generating perverse and unintended consequences that fuel calls for even more law enforcement.

In the next chapter I provide a broad overview of the practice of smuggling and the paradoxical nature of its double-edged relationship to the state. This underside of cross-border economic exchange has symbiotically interacted with state practices. Although law-enforcing state actors and law-evading smugglers have grown up in opposition to each other, I emphasize the multiple ways in which the two groups have also very much depended on the other.

In chapter 3 I turn to the specific dynamics of policing and smuggling across the U.S.-Mexico border. The border has always been marked by persistent, widespread, and diverse smuggling activities in both northward and southward directions. Largely because of the feedback effects of state policies on both sides of the border, however, the northbound flows of drugs and migrants eventually became the more prominent and contro-versial components of the clandestine side of the U.S.-Mexico economic relationship. In other words, state practices, rather than simply abstract "market forces," have been essential in creating Mexico's competitive ad-vantage as a major exporter of both illegal drugs and illegal labor to the U.S. market and in setting up the political conditions for the sharp escala-tion of control efforts in recent years.

In chapter 4 I trace the expansion of U.S. and Mexican efforts to police the smuggling of drugs across the border from the late 1980s to the late 1990s. As an unintended consequence of U.S. efforts to interdict the smuggling of Colombian cocaine through the Caribbean, the cocaine flow was pushed to the U.S.-Mexico border at the same time as the United States and Mexico were beginning to forge a new and more intimate economic partnership. To help secure the smooth passage of NAFTA, U.S. and Mex-ican leaders orchestrated a law enforcement buildup on both sides of the border which signaled a joint commitment to drug control. Highly visible but misleading indicators of state resolve—increased arrests, drug sei-zures, bilateral initiatives—helped sustain an image of cooperation and progress and obscured the failings, flaws, and negative side effects of the enforcement effort.

This positive image was sustained long enough for the free trade accord to pass, but the unintended feedback effects of both enhanced law enforcement and NAFTA itself generated new problems that threatened to undermine bilateral relations. First, increased Mexican law enforcement perversely created greater opportunities for officials to collect bribes and pay-offs. And, this in turn attracted more intensive U.S. media and congressional scrutiny. Second, the post-NAFTA boom in commercial flows simultaneously drew more political attention to the border and made the task of weeding out the drug flow increasingly difficult. This politically embarrassing situation created an opening for opportunistic lawmakers and law enforcers to simplistically blame the free trade accord for the failures of drug control and to push for even more drug interdiction resources. Scrambling to manage these policy feedback effects, U.S. and Mexican officials turned to more high-tech and militarized forms of drug enforcement.

Chapter 5 mirrors chapter 4 but focuses on intensified U.S. efforts to police the cross-border flow of illegal Mexican migrants in the 1990s. Past state practices helped create the conditions for a domestic backlash against illegal immigration in the early 1990s (especially in the border state of California, which was hit hard by an economic recession and budget crisis partly induced by the post–Cold War retrenchment of the defense industry). Skillfully exploiting dramatic images of illegal immigrants rushing across the border, political entrepreneurs targeted the border as both the source of the illegal immigration problem and the most appropriate site of the policing solution (rather than, for example, the workplace). Once the border became the primary stage on which the government's moral resolve to combat illegal immigration would be tested, politicians from across the political spectrum scrambled to outdo one another in proposing tougher measures to secure the border. In this heated political climate, the federal government launched a high-profile border control campaign that focused on fortifying the most visible and popular urban entry points for illegal migrants, pushing them to attempt the clandestine crossing in more remote areas farther from public and media attention.

An enabling political climate and bureaucratic entrepreneurialism were essential in sparking this border offensive, but the enforcement campaign has subsequently taken on a life of its own. By prompting shifts in the methods and location of illegal border crossings, law enforcement has created more (and more challenging) work for itself. As migrants have been forced to rely more on the help of professional smugglers, law enforcement has responded with tougher and more expansive antismuggling initiatives. Similarly, as migrants have been pushed to attempt the border crossing in more remote areas, the reach of law enforcement has had to geographically expand. Even though the border enforcement effort has failed to substantially reduce the flow of migrants and has had the side effect of making organized migrant smuggling a much more profitable business, it has succeeded in making illegal border crossings less visible and more dispersed—and thus in projecting an image of a more secure and orderly border.

To broaden the analysis and draw comparative conclusions, chapter 6 examines the forms of police escalation on the external borders of the European Union, focusing on the boundaries between Spain and Morocco and between Germany and Poland. While I identify a general pattern of law enforcement escalation across these EU borders and the U.S.-Mexico border, I also point to important variations in the focus, intensity, and strategies of border policing, the messages and images it communicates, and the audiences to whom these are communicated. German and Spanish policies are embedded in a regional framework that shapes both the politics and practice of border enforcement. Thus, whereas the escalation of U.S. immigration control along the U.S.-Mexico border represents a unilateral reassertion of national sovereignty, and the escalation of U.S. and Mexican drug control represents a U.S.-driven bilateral effort to harden both sides of the border, the escalation of law enforcement across these external borders of the European Union reflects a multilateral "pooling of sovereignty" and the creation of "buffer zones" to insulate an integrating Western Europe.

In the concluding chapter I reexamine the central claims of the book and highlight some theoretical and policy implications. The escalation of territorial policing, I suggest, offers lessons for the study of borders and the practice of regulating border crossings.

CHAPTER TWO

The Political Economy of Global Smuggling

Smuggling consists of all cross-border economic activity that is unauthorized by either the receiving or the sending country. Although the story of the emergence and growth of the global economy is well known, this clandestine side has received far less attention. In one form or another, smuggling has existed as long as there have been restrictions on cross-border economic exchange.[1] It is important to keep in mind, however, that although the total volume and profitability of smuggling may be much higher today than ever before, as a percentage of overall global economic activity it is possibly no more (and very possibly much less) significant than in the past. What has changed over time are the particular smuggling activities, the structure of the smuggling organizations, methods (and speed) of transport, state laws and the intensity of their enforcement, the degree of societal anxiety and political attention, and the level of consumer demand.

THE BUSINESS OF SMUGGLING

The business of smuggling is extraordinarily diverse. Today it includes trafficking in hazardous waste and chlorofluorocarbons (CFCs), arms,

1. The word *smuggler* apparently emerged during the English civil wars, 1642–49. A royal proclamation was announced in 1661 "for the prevention and punishment of all frauds on the Customs committed by . . . a sort of lewd people called 'smuckellors,' never heard of before the late disordered times, who make it their trade . . . to steal and defraud His Majesty of His Customs." Quoted in Geoffrey Morley, *The Smuggling War: The Government's Fight against Smuggling in the 18th and 19th Centuries* (Stroud, Gloucestershire: Alan Sutton, 1994), 4.

nuclear material, antiquities, precious stones and metals, banned psychoactive substances (such as heroin and cocaine), money, pornography, and animals and animal products. And, of course, there is the booming business of human smuggling, itself a diverse enterprise involving the trafficking in migrants, prostitutes, babies, and even body parts (thanks to modern technologies that make it possible to store and ship high-demand organs such as kidneys and livers).

The economic importance of smuggling—although impossible to calculate with precision and often ignored in official records—is clearly enormous. Estimates of the global value of drug smuggling range from $180 billion to over $300 billion in annual retail sales, making it one of the world's largest industries.[2] Transporting illegal migrants into industrialized countries has developed into a multibillion-dollar business, with smugglers charging individuals up to $50,000 for their clandestine travel services.[3] The remittances sent home by illegal migrants provide a critical source of foreign exchange for many debt-strapped developing countries.[4] The smuggling of endangered species is estimated to be a $10 billion trade.[5] These various smuggling practices contribute to massive money laundering, tax evasion, and capital flight. The International Monetary Fund (IMF) calculates that $500 billion is laundered annually through the global financial system.[6]

The United States is by far the world's number one smuggling target, with illegal drugs and migrants leading the list of imports. The United States is also probably the single largest exporter of smuggled goods if one considers, for example, the mass quantities of American cigarettes, pornographic material, money, weapons, and stolen cars that are smuggled out of the country every year. Most of the attention, not surprisingly, is on what is coming into the country rather than on what is going out. For example, complaints by Mexico that large quantities of illegal weapons from the United States end up south of the border in violation of Mexican gun control laws generate relatively little U.S. media coverage or concern among Washington policymakers (particularly in comparison with the concern over the influx of drugs and immigrants). Similarly, while Mexico

2. Paul B. Stares, *Global Habit: The Drug Problem in a Borderless World* (Washington, D.C.: Brookings Institution, 1996), 2, 123–24.

3. The International Organization for Migration estimates that 4 million migrants are smuggled every year in a global trade valued at $10 billion: *Migration News,* August 1999.

4. Remittances from both legal and illegal migrants are a leading source of foreign exchange for a broad range of countries, including Mexico, El Salvador, the Dominican Republic, Morocco, and the Philippines.

5. Donovan Webster, "The Animal Smugglers," *New York Times Magazine,* 16 February 1997, 27.

6. International Monetary Fund, "Tougher Measures Needed to Counter Macro Effects of Money Laundering," *IMF Survey,* 29 July 1996, 246.

is chastised for being a key transshipment point for Colombian cocaine bound for the U.S. market, largely ignored is the fact that the United States is a major transshipment point for cocaine exported to Canada.

Laws and consumer demand are the most basic determinants of what smugglers smuggle. For example, a world of high tariffs encourages clandestine trade in legal commodities to avoid import or export duties. This kind of smuggling has been a well-entrenched practice since before the founding of the United States.[7] Loss of revenue from duties has long been a major national concern, since U.S. customs duties were virtually the federal government's only source of revenue for much of the nation's history. As recently as the eve of World War I, approximately half of all federal revenue was still generated through duties.[8]

In a world of low tariffs, on the other hand, smuggling tends to shift from evading tariffs on legal commodities to evading prohibitions on commodities deemed undesirable. Still, even in a world of low tariffs, variations in domestic taxes and prices on some high-demand legal products, such as cigarettes, alcohol, and pharmaceutical drugs, provide enormous incentives for smuggling. For example, many Americans visiting Mexican border towns illegally bring back pharmaceuticals.[9] At the same time, mass quantities of a highly addictive legal drug (tobacco) are smuggled out of the United States—for example, to Canada, where cigarette taxes are much higher.[10] Similarly, German law enforcement officials worry not only about the smuggling of illegal drugs across the country's eastern border but also about the mass smuggling of untaxed cigarettes. Another important but too often overlooked type of smuggling that persists in a low-tariff environment is the smuggling of legal commodities that are obtained illegally, such as stolen cars and computer chips. There is a multibillion-dollar cross-border trade in stolen cars, which are among the leading smuggled commodities that move from richer to poorer countries.

As the trend toward an open global trading system continues, prohibitions rather than tariffs and quotas increasingly shape the business of smuggling, for accompanying a general liberalization of trade is an increase in the selective criminalization of trade. Some prohibitions, such as

7. See John W. Tyler, *Smugglers and Patriots: Boston Merchants and the Advent of the American Revolution* (Boston: Northeastern University Press, 1986).

8. Laurence Frederick Schmeckebier, *The Customs Service: Its History, Activities, and Organization* (Baltimore: Johns Hopkins University Press, 1924), 2.

9. Dana Calvo, "Frontier Medicine: Tijuana Postcard," *New Republic* 217, no. 25 (1997): 15–17.

10. Sometimes such smuggling includes the collusion of the manufacturer. A unit of the RJR Nabisco Holdings Corporation pleaded guilty in December 1998 to federal criminal charges of smuggling cigarettes into Canada via an Indian reservation along the border in upstate New York, and agreed to pay $15 million in penalties: *New York Times*, 23 December 1998.

those against heroin and cocaine, are almost universal. Others are more nation-specific: variations in attempts to control the trade in pornographic material shows that one nation's tolerated pleasure may be another nation's abominable vice. For instance, although American entertainment products are legally promoted and consumed across much of the globe, the smuggling of forbidden American videotapes into Iran is a lucrative business, just as it was in the Soviet bloc before the fall of the Iron Curtain. Even the illegal use of satellite dishes in China is an electronic means of smuggling in American entertainment products.

The lack of broad agreement on many prohibitions undermines their effectiveness, but even when a degree of consensus exists, there remains enormous variation in how (and how much) it is enforced. Notice the differences in national drug laws and their enforcement despite the existence of a global drug prohibition regime.[11] Thus, the approach to regulating drugs in Holland is less punitive than in the United States, but U.S. laws are far less punitive than those in Indonesia. These variations can create significant tensions between states, as well as both opportunities and constraints for smugglers.

Moreover, depending on the political winds and social norms of the day, what is illegitimate trade in one era may be legitimate trade in another. Contrast the American regulatory approach toward alcohol today and the prohibitionist approach of the 1920s; today's prohibitionist approach toward cocaine and opium products and the free-market approach of a century ago; today's global prohibition against the slave trade and the legal trade in slaves in previous centuries. Prohibitions against money laundering and trafficking in endangered species were nonexistent even a few decades ago.

Just as some countries and regions occupy a special niche in legal trade, so too do different countries and regions have a niche in illegal trade. The industrialized countries dominate legal trade; illegal trade is an area of significant comparative advantage for many developing countries. This awkward and sobering reality is not, of course, always recognized by the leading international institutions (such as the IMF, the World Bank, and the World Trade Organization) that monitor global trade patterns and urge developing countries to specialize on the basis of the principles of comparative advantage.

Thus, asparagus is officially listed as Peru's most important agricultural export, but coca products are unofficially the country's number one export. Illegal drugs are the most important export for a number of countries across the Western Hemisphere, Africa, and Asia. Yet though drugs

---

11. Ethan Nadelmann, "Global Prohibition Regimes: The Evolution of Norms in International Society," *International Organization* 44, no. 4 (1990): 427–526.

are the single most important smuggled commodity worldwide, for many countries the importance of smuggling extends well beyond the drug trade. Madagascar, for instance, is on the extreme periphery of the legal global economy but is a key player in the massive clandestine trade in endangered species, such as rare turtles and snakes, of which the United States is a major importer.[12] South Africa's dominance in the diamond trade is well known; much less recognized is its dominance in the illegal rhino horn and ivory trade.[13] Russia, China, and Brazil are leading exporters of smuggled gold.[14] Developing countries also have a comparative advantage in the export of low-wage workers, many of whom are prohibited in the countries they enter. El Salvador, for example, has exported to the United States a significant percentage of its labor force, which in turn generates crucial foreign exchange for the Salvadoran economy through remittances. Other countries specialize in transshipment: Panama is a free-trade zone not only for legitimate trade but for an enormous amount of the illegitimate movement of money, weapons, and people. Many of the Chinese smuggled to the United States are routed through Panama to purchase false travel documents.[15] Paraguay too has long been a major smuggling transshipment hub, a distribution center for the smuggling of American cigarettes and other products into South America.[16]

The economic importance of smuggling demonstrates that there is not just a formal, aboveground dimension of regional and global interdependence but an informal, underground dimension as well. For some countries, it is the smuggling-based part of the economy that is most responsive to (and integrated into) global markets. Moreover, smuggling provides an alternative avenue of upward mobility for entrepreneurial but marginalized social groups that have little access to legitimate business opportunities. And upward mobility through illegal trade may provide a mechanism for some groups to break into more legitimate trade—which can also provide a cover for illegitimate trade.

Advances in technology and global transportation networks have dramatically reduced the time and cost of smuggling. Historically, waterways provided its primary channel; then the development of road and rail networks considerably expanded the smuggler's options, as did the arrival of the automobile. Today, the traditional land and sea routes of previous

12. Webster, "Animal Smugglers."

13. De Wet Potgieter, *Contraband: South Africa and the International Trade in Ivory and Rhino Horn* (Cape Town: Queillerie, 1995).

14. R. T. Naylor, "The Underworld of Gold," *Crime, Law, and Social Change* 25 (1996): 191–241.

15. *Washington Post*, 23 October 1995; *Miami Herald*, 8 August 1999.

16. Jorge Domínguez, "Smuggling," *Foreign Policy* 20 (fall 1975): 87–96, 161–64.

eras remain essential, but growing access to airspace and now cyberspace (for example, in the transfer of intellectual property and pornography via the Internet) has further expanded the possibilities and opportunities for smuggling. Literally anything that crosses a national border can be used for smuggling, from the most common and conventional (car trunks, luggage) to the most desperate and dangerous (the human stomach) to the most ingenious (baby diapers or jalapeño peppers) to the most unstoppable (the airwaves).

But although the methods are as diverse as the commodities, most smuggling parallels the methods and routes of legal commerce. States consequently face an increasingly awkward but unavoidable predicament: policy measures that facilitate the flow of legal trade (improved transportation systems, trade liberalization, deregulation of shipping, privatization of ports, and so on) can unintentionally facilitate illegal trade as well. Furthermore, as the speed and volume of trade continues to increase (from the mid-1980s to the mid-1990s world exports doubled to $4.1 trillion), so too does the difficulty of weeding out the illegal from the legal.

There is significant variation in the ease of smuggling. Successful evasion of state control efforts is shaped by differences in the expertise and resources needed, the means of concealment, and the willingness of victims to report the activity to state authorities.[17] Drug smuggling is thus more difficult to control than slave trading. Controls are likely to be most effective where supply of the commodity is limited and transport cumbersome (and sometimes dangerous, as in the smuggling of nuclear material). Legal market alternatives may also increase the relative effectiveness of controls (for example, there are legal disposal alternatives to the cross-border dumping of toxic waste). So do variations in consumer demand: an animal collector buying a smuggled parrot presents a kind of demand different from that of an addict buying smuggled heroin. It is in the drug case, not surprisingly, that state controls are less effective—but within the drug trade itself there are differences: border interdiction is more effective against marijuana imports than heroin and cocaine imports because marijuana is a bulkier product.

To classify all smuggling as a form of organized crime is highly misleading, given the extreme variation in the level of organization and the degree of criminality. How organized and how criminal smuggling is depends on what is being smuggled and the intensity and form of state control efforts. Today's smugglers range from self-smugglers (such as illegal immigrants) to individuals smuggling goods for their own personal consumption (for example, American tourists bringing home Cuban cigars) to independent, small-scale entrepreneurs, loose networks of trans-

17. Nadelmann, "Global Prohibition Regimes," 510.

national gangs, and highly developed and sophisticated criminal organizations. Even though the global reach of some smuggling groups has accelerated with the integration of the global economy, the image of an octopuslike global network of crime syndicates that runs the criminal underworld through its expansive tentacles is a fiction invented by sensationalistic journalists and opportunistic politicians. If this picture matched reality, the challenge to law enforcement would actually be far less serious: one would need only to cut off the octopus head, and the tentacles would die with it. What makes putting smugglers out of business so difficult is not only that there are so many heads in so many places but that every time one head is cut off, a replacement head grows back: that is, every time one smuggling location or method is closed down by law enforcement, another one emerges. Law enforcement can deter and even eliminate individual smugglers and smuggling organizations, but doing so rarely leads to a significant and extended reduction in smuggling.

Smugglers are in many respects similar to their counterparts in legitimate businesses: they engage in some rather conventional business practices, such as subcontracting, joint ventures and strategic alliances, use of offshore bank accounts, diversification through investment in various sectors of the economy, and of course, the use of money and influence to gain government favor. Not surprisingly, many smugglers view their activities simply as a business that happens to be illegal. They would no doubt agree with Adam Smith's contention that "a smuggler is a person who, although no doubt blamable for violating the laws of the country, is frequently incapable of violating those of natural justice, and would have been, in every respect, an excellent citizen had not the laws of his country made that a crime which Nature never meant to be so."[18]

Yet if smuggling is an economic activity like any other, it is also unlike any other. Its illegal nature gives it some unique characteristics. For one thing, disputes between smugglers are sometimes resolved by killing rather than suing each other. For another, high profits are as much a product of laws and law enforcement as they are of market demand, for the peculiar nature of smuggling is largely a product of its relationship to the state.

THE INTERDEPENDENCE OF SMUGGLING AND THE STATE

It is tempting simply to interpret the evasion of state controls through smuggling as alarming evidence of the growing incapacity of the state to control its borders. A broader historical perspective, however, makes it clear that the limits of state controls are nothing new. With rare exceptions,

18. Quoted in Domínguez, "Smuggling," 164.

borders have always been fairly porous. There never was a time when state control over transborder flows "was assured or secure."[19] Effective border regulations have long been more myth than reality, a political construct providing an appearance of control which helps to prop up the state's territorial legitimacy. Moreover, the capacity of the state to control its borders is in many respects higher now than during most of the history of the modern state. Comprehensive border controls are a relatively recent invention.[20] The creation of the passport, for example, emerged only as a by-product of World War I. It should also be noted that until this century, few countries even attempted to prohibit many of the cross-border economic activities that are today perceived as challenges to the state, such as drug trafficking, and the criminalization of activities such as money laundering is even more recent.

In this regard, it is important to distinguish between authority and control as interrelated dimensions of state power. As Janice Thomson explains, states claim meta-political authority: the right to decide what is political and, as such, subject to state coercion.[21] But the authority to make rules differs from the ability to enforce them. When state actors invoke metapolitical authority in criminalizing specific economic practices, the gap between the state's authority to create prohibition laws and its ability to enforce such laws fully is the space where smuggling takes place. Put another way, smuggling is defined by and depends on the state's exercising its metapolitical authority to criminalize without the full capacity or willingness to enforce its laws. Even to talk about cross-border smuggling makes little sense outside the context of an interstate system in which states claim the authority to grant or deny legal territorial access.[22]

Thus, the state-smuggler relationship is a paradoxical one, defined by irony and contradiction. The smuggler is pursued by the state but at the same time is kept in business by the state. The smuggler is dependent on the state in multiple ways. The most obvious but essential point is that state laws provide the very opening for (and high profitability of) smuggling in the first place. In this sense, states create the incentives for smugglers. And although prohibitions and efforts to enforce them generally fail to eliminate the targeted activity, in practice they function as a peculiar form of

19. Janice Thomson, "State Sovereignty in International Relations: Bridging the Gap between Theory and Empirical Research," *International Studies Quarterly* 39, no. 2 (1995): 216.

20. See John Torpey, "States and the Regulation of Migration in the 20th Century North Atlantic World," in *The Wall around the West: State Borders and Immigration Controls in North America and Europe,* ed. Peter Andreas and Timothy Snyder (Lantham, Md.: Rowman and Littlefield, 2000).

21. Thomson, "State Sovereignty."

22. See Stephen Krasner, "Power Politics, Institutions, and Transnational Relations," in *Bringing Transnational Relations Back In: Non-State Actors, Domestic Structures, and International Institutions,* ed. Thomas Risse-Kappen (New York: Cambridge University Press, 1995).

regulation. The method, intensity, and focus of law enforcement shapes the location and form of smuggling, the size and structure of the smuggling organizations, and the cost and profitability of smuggling.

The transformation of migrant smuggling through Central America in recent years illustrates how law enforcement can powerfully shape (even while failing to control) such activity. The International Organization for Migration reports that "as authorities in the region stepped up the border control and enforcement efforts, migrant traffickers have had to grow in sophistication in order to survive. Links to transnational crime syndicates have consequently been established."[23] Even the U.S. officials pushing for more intensive enforcement warn that "as enforcement efforts become more effective . . . we can expect the smugglers to become more sophisticated and hard-core criminal groups to become involved in this extremely lucrative trade."[24] Thus, not only do smugglers depend on state laws for their existence, but the enforcement of such laws often creates better organized and more skillful smuggling groups, sometimes unintentionally (but predictably) turning disorganized into organized smuggling.

The state shapes the business of smuggling not only through its power to criminalize but also through its power to liberalize. For example, peasant farmers displaced by market-based reforms have an increased incentive to choose an underground "exit option" of becoming either illegal immigrants or producers of illegal drug crops. Market liberalization and deregulation can also influence the methods of smuggling. For example, the deregulation of transportation can facilitate the use of commercial cargo conveyances by smugglers. The free-trade agreements that promote cross-border commerce can in turn provide a convenient cover for smugglers, who increasingly conceal their illegitimate cargo within legitimate cargo. Likewise, the deregulation of financial systems to woo foreign capital can facilitate the laundering of profits from smuggling.[25]

Laws and their enforcement also mean that smugglers necessarily interact symbiotically with elements of the state apparatus. Some smugglers attempt to intimidate or violently neutralize state law enforcers, but the general rule is to buy off officials. In doing so, smugglers purchase a key service monopolized by the state: the nonenforcement of the law. Cor-

23. International Organization for Migration, "Trafficking in Migrants: Some Global and Regional Perspectives" (paper submitted to Regional Conference on Migration, Puebla, Mexico, 13–14 March 1996), 5.

24. Interagency Working Group, *Presidential Initiative to Deter Alien Smuggling: Report of the Interagency Working Group* (Washington, D.C., December 1995).

25. In the case of Mexico, see Peter Andreas, "When Policies Collide: Market Reform, Market Prohibition, and the Narcotization of the Mexican Economy," in *The Illicit Global Economy and State Power,* ed. H. Richard Friman and Peter Andreas (Lanham, Md.: Rowman & Littlefield, 1999).

ruption, in the form of bribes and payoffs, functions as a kind of informal tax on smuggling and is viewed by the smuggler as a necessary (however costly) business expense. As law enforcement pressure increases, so too does the corruption tax. Moreover, smugglers may rely on corrupt officials not only to ensure that their operations are not targeted by enforcement but to provide protection against (or to eliminate) rival smugglers or even against other state authorities (with the result that different police agencies sometimes shoot at each other).

Corrupt officials provide other essential services as well, such as the fraudulent documents (passports, visas, naturalization cards) that facilitate, most notably, migrant smuggling. Document selling is an enormous business throughout Central America, the primary passageway for the smuggling of Chinese immigrants to the United States.[26] Corruption scandals involving migrant smuggling have led to the replacement of immigration directors in Panama, Guatemala, and Belize.[27]

Corruption thus suggests both the power and limits of the state: on the one hand, it reflects the penetration *of* the state; on the other hand, it reflects the penetration *by* the state. When pressured by the state, most smugglers simply wish to evade rather than attack or even overtly challenge the state. Of course, one must not dismiss or belittle the serious threat that smugglers can pose to state institutions and to the rule of law. Indeed, in some notorious cases, smuggling and the state virtually merge so that the illegal activity becomes a state-sponsored enterprise. The Garcia Meza regime in Bolivia and the Noriega regime in Panama are particularly infamous examples.

Just as smugglers depend on the state, so too the state may depend on smugglers, although in a much different sense. This dependence takes multiple forms. Economic dependence can be significant: in Latin American drug-exporting countries such as Peru and Bolivia, the foreign exchange generated by smuggling enters the cash-starved financial system through the central bank (which in turn boosts foreign exchange reserves and helps service the foreign debt), while the jobs generated by smuggling cushion the unemployment crisis and other social dislocations created by economic restructuring. Regardless of how sincere and intense the government's battle against drug smuggling may be, the immediate economic repercussions of suddenly winning the battle would be severe.[28]

A different form of economic dependence is generated through corruption. Interestingly, while the response to corruption in regulating the

26. *Washington Post*, 23 October 1995.
27. Interagency Working Group, *Presidential Initiative*.
28. See R. T. Naylor, *Hot Money and the Politics of Debt* (New York: Simon & Schuster, 1987).

legal economy in many developing countries has been to reduce state intervention, the response to corruption in regulating the illegal smuggling
economy is to increase state intervention. Consequently, the corrupt practices that market-based reforms were designed to curb in the legal economy are thriving in the illegal economy.

Beyond corruption, however, it is important to emphasize that there are
also legal channels through which resources from smuggling are directly
transferred to the state, most notably asset forfeiture laws. In the United
States, asset forfeiture has turned drug control (and anti-organized crime
initiatives in general) into an enormous revenue-generating activity for
law enforcement. For example, between 1985 and 1991 the Department
of Justice confiscated more than $1.5 billion in illegal assets, and almost
double this amount between 1991 and 1996. Asset forfeiture has become
such an integral dimension of drug law enforcement that as former Attorney General Dick Thornburgh pointed out, "It's now possible for a drug
dealer to serve time in a forfeiture-financed prison after having been arrested by agents driving a forfeiture-provided automobile while working
in a forfeiture-funded sting operation."[29] In 1998 the INS seized 26,974
vehicles used by smugglers along the Mexico border. Total border vehicle
seizures that year generated $42 million for the federal government.[30]

State officials also depend on individual smugglers to carry out their
antismuggling mission. Law enforcement cannot do its job without at least
minimal assistance from smugglers, for they are the most important source
of information on smuggling, and to obtain this information, officials must
constantly bargain and negotiate with them. A number of drug smugglers,
for example, received lenient sentences for providing information that led
to the sentencing of Noriega by a Florida jury. At a lower and less publicized level this sort of bargaining is standard operating procedure, blur-
ring the line between legality and illegality. Law enforcement officials may
overlook the activities of one smuggler in exchange for information that
leads to the capture of other smugglers.

Ultimately, it is the very persistence of smuggling, and the perception of
it as a growing threat, that is most critical to the persistence of law enforcement. In other words, even though law enforcement fails to deter the business of smuggling (and in some ways helps sustain it), smuggling keeps law
enforcement in business. This is particularly important in an era of aus-
terity, shrinking budgets, and antistatist ideology. In many countries the
growth of law enforcement is the most prominent exception to the gen-

29. Quoted in Eric Blumenson and Eva Nilsen, "The Drug War's Hidden Economic
Agenda (Seizing the Property of Drug Dealers)," *Nation* 226 (March 1998): 11–16.
30. Associated Press, 12 July 1999.

eral retreat of the state. In some cases, security and intelligence agencies initially designed to deter military attacks have embraced antismuggling tasks. Retooling old security institutions for new security missions can be awkward and expensive, but bureaucratic incentives and political pressures continue to push in this direction.

As long as state restrictions on cross-border flows have existed, there has been smuggling, and, absent the emergence of a truly border-free global economy, there always will be. Through their interaction on and across national borders, states and smugglers have not only challenged but reinforced each other in multiple ways.[31] This peculiar relationship has varied across time and smuggling activity, as have the outcomes that emerge from it. The game between law enforcers and law-evading smugglers is never entirely won or lost, but the playing has intensified in recent years. The following chapters explain how and why this has happened in the case of policing the smuggling of drugs and migrants across the U.S.-Mexico border.

31. This is an example of the interdependence of rule breakers and rule enforcers as described in Gary T. Marx, "Ironies of Social Control: Authorities as Contributors to Deviance through Escalation, Nonenforcement, and Covert Facilitation," *Social Problems* 28, no. 3 (1991): 221–46.

Part II

Policing and Smuggling across the U.S.-Mexico Border

CHAPTER THREE

Creating the Clandestine Side
of the Border Economy

The popular notion that the U.S.-Mexico border is out of control falsely
assumes that there was once a time when it was truly under control. Even
though the smuggling of drugs and migrants has received the most media
and policy attention in recent years, it should be emphasized that these
clandestine activities are part of an old and diverse border smuggling
economy that thrived long before drugs and migrants were being smuggled. As Peter Reuter and David Ronfeldt have noted, "Mexicans have always been available to supply whatever Americans want but cannot obtain
legally in their own country—just as Americans have always been ready to
provide whatever Mexicans want and cannot acquire readily in Mexico."[1]
Paralleling the historical process of formal economic integration between
the United States and Mexico has been an informal (and certainly less celebrated) process of clandestine economic integration.

THE DIVERSITY OF SMUGGLING

It is important to point out the wide range of smuggling practices that
have been an integral dimension of cross-border economic exchange since
the nineteenth century. In fact, the U.S.-Mexico economic relationship
was founded on smuggling—and unlike the situation today, most of what
was smuggled flowed from north to south. High tariffs and minimal enforcement capacity meant that a majority of Mexico's trade following in-

1. Peter Reuter and David Ronfeldt, *Quest for Integrity: The Mexican-U.S. Drug Issue in the
1980s* (Santa Monica, Calif.: RAND Corporation, 1991), 10.

dependence in 1821 was contraband. In the 1820s two-thirds of the foreign goods entering the country had evaded customs duties.[2] Smuggling into Mexico from the United States reached extreme levels in the following decades. With the ending of the Mexican-American War in 1848, trade with Texas rose sharply—much of it in the form of smuggling. The United States also became a major clandestine exporter of arms to Mexico, a business that was especially lucrative in periods of Mexican political and social unrest (and continues to thrive today). During the American Civil War, Mexico also functioned as a back door through which to smuggle confederate cotton to Europe. Also, until the end of the Civil War, thousands of fugitive slaves smuggled themselves across the border (leading to many incursions into Mexican territory by U.S. law enforcement).[3]

A boom in smuggling—and in the policing of smuggling—was fueled by the introduction of alcohol prohibition in the United States in the 1920s. The size of the U.S. Customs force was small until the prohibition era, when the number of inspectors along the border rose from 111 in 1925 to 723 in 1930.[4] Many Mexican border towns rapidly expanded in the process of facilitating the illicit liquor trade, leading to the creation of an extensive border-smuggling infrastructure. After repeal, this infrastructure simply adapted to other smuggling activities. At the same time, prohibition had helped establish a much greater (even if still limited) federal policing presence along the border.

Meanwhile, the smuggling of legal goods into Mexico, which was the backbone of smuggling in the nineteenth century, continued on a massive scale in the twentieth. In the 1920s Mexican officials even contemplated building fences around some border towns to keep out goods smuggled from the United States; the governor of Baja, however, protested that this would give the residents of these towns "the appearance of herded cattle."[5] The building of fences to control illegal cross-border flows would later become a popular strategy on the U.S. side of the border.

Although U.S. border states historically enjoyed a significant comparative advantage in the contraband trade, the flow was certainly not entirely one way. For example, the smuggling of candelilla, a strong natural wax from native shrubs, had become a thriving export business in some northern Mexican states by the 1950s, thanks to the strict controls on price and

2. Jorge A. Hernández, "Trading across the Border: National Customs Guards in Nuevo Leon," *Southwestern Historical Quarterly* 100, no. 4 (1997): 433–51.

3. Ethan Nadelmann, *Cops across Borders: The Internationalization of U.S. Criminal Law Enforcement* (University Park: Pennsylvania State University Press, 1993).

4. Ibid., 30.

5. Marshall Carter, "The Political Economy of Crime in the U.S.-Mexican Borderlands" (revision of a paper prepared for the North American Economic Studies Association, Southern Economics Association Meeting, Washington, D.C., November 1978), 6.

production imposed by the central government. Also, the illegal trade in animals from Mexico has for decades been so profitable a business—especially the smuggling of parrots, often intoxicated with tequila to keep them quiet—that feuds between rival smugglers could result in their hijacking one another's parrot shipments.[6] Endangered species legislation has created further incentives for animal smuggling. Even the illegal importation of insects from Mexico—fueled by the demands of insect collectors in the United States and elsewhere—has evolved into a sizable business. One smuggler arrested in 1995, for example, had been bringing tens of thousands of Mexican beetles, moths, and butterflies into the United States for over a decade and selling them for as much as $1,000 apiece.[7]

Years of protectionist Mexican economic policies meant that U.S. border towns functioned as unofficial shopping centers for merchandise to be smuggled into Mexico. In the late 1970s, Mexicans purchased so much in Laredo, Texas, that even though the local residents earned among the lowest wages in the country, Laredo was ranked among the highest cities in retail sales per capita. Of the $4 million worth of television sets exported from Laredo to Mexico in 1978, an estimated $2.8 million worth were smuggled. The Laredo airport became a major hub for small planes loaded with smuggled U.S. goods bound for Mexico. Flying was not only faster but cheaper: going by land required passing through more Mexican customs check-points, and therefore spending more on payoffs.[8]

In February 1979 the López Portillo administration appealed to the Carter administration for assistance in stemming the contraband trade in luxury items, electronics and other appliances, powdered milk, and more, which was estimated to have cost Mexican business $1 billion in losses.[9] In 1977, Mexican dairymen blamed a loss of over $400,000 per day on smuggled U.S. milk.[10] Only membership in the General Agreement on Tariffs and Trade (GATT) in 1986 and the subsequent liberalization of trade (formalized by NAFTA in 1994) enabled Mexico to substantially undermine this kind of smuggling. But just as smugglers who made their living from contraband saw their business shrink because of the state's market liberalization policies, the lack of liberalization in other key sectors of the clandestine economic relationship—most notably drugs and

6. See Timothy Green, *The Smugglers: An Investigation into the World of the Contemporary Smuggler* (New York: Walker, 1969), 292.

7. *Houston Chronicle,* 20 July 1995.

8. Tom Miller, *On the Border* (New York: Harper & Row, 1981), 52.

9. Marshall Carter, "Law, Order, and the Border: El Paso Del Norte" (revision of a paper prepared for the annual meeting of the National Council on Geographic Education, Mexico City, November 1979), 6.

10. Carter, "Political Economy of Crime," 17.

migrant labor—assured not only the persistence but expansion of the smuggling networks built up over a long history of protectionist economic policies.

MIGRANT SMUGGLING

A century and a half ago, Mexico tried unsuccessfully to curb illegal U.S. immigration into its northern regions. The so-called Mexican Decree of 3 April 1830 had prohibited immigration from the United States, and Mexico deployed garrisons to try to enforce the law. Even the battle at the Alamo was, in a sense, a bloody attempt to control illegal American immigration. Mexico won that battle but lost the war. After the Treaty of Guadalupe Hidalgo of 1848 and the Gadsden Purchase of 1853, the regions in question became part of the sovereign territory of the United States, and white settlers—many of them European immigrants—moved west to occupy the newly acquired lands. Today the migration movement has been reversed, with vast numbers of Mexicans populating these regions.

The first U.S. attempt to control migration across the southwest border was directed not at Mexicans but at Chinese laborers: an unintended consequence of the Chinese Exclusion Act of 1882 had been to turn Mexico into the primary conduit for smuggling Chinese into the United States. Chinese migrants, debarking south of the California-Mexico border at Ensenada, Guaymas, or Mazatlán, would pay five dollars to be transported to the borderline, and then up to forty dollars to be smuggled into southern California.[11] Some traveled farther into the Mexican interior and were then smuggled across the border between Juárez and El Paso. In response, federal law enforcement officials (called "Chinese inspectors") were dispatched to the border to curb the practice.

Despite an 1885 law restricting the importation of contract workers, large numbers of Mexicans were informally recruited by U.S. employers to work in southwestern agriculture in the early twentieth century. Whereas formal, legal entry was a complicated process, crossing the border illegally was relatively simple and largely overlooked. Up to half a million Mexicans may have come to the United States in the first decade of the century. The Mexican Revolution, U.S. labor shortages during World War I, and the continued expansion of agriculture in the Southwest fueled a further influx. Restrictions on European immigration in 1921 and 1924 also had the unintended effect of turning the U.S.-Mexico border into a conduit for illegal European immigrants. By the time the U.S. Border Patrol was

---

11. Leon C. Metz, *Border: The U.S.-Mexico Line* (El Paso, Tex.: Mangan, 1989), 365.

formed in 1924, with a $1 million budget and a total force of some 450 officers, the primary targets along the southwestern border were Europeans and Asians (although the Border Patrol in those prohibition years also spent much of its time pursuing alcohol smugglers).

Strict controls against Mexicans crossing the border were widely perceived as neither viable nor desirable. As one observer put it, "from a practical administrative standpoint a quota system would be impossible to enforce" because the long border with Mexico "could not be adequately policed. The pressure to bring Mexicans across the border would be so great and smuggling them would become so profitable that a quota law for Mexicans would become a joke."[12] As a substitute for the reduction in European and Asian workers, Mexicans were viewed by employers and policymakers alike as an ideal labor force: flexible, compliant, and temporary (or so it seemed at the time). When they were no longer needed, many were simply deported. Hundreds of thousands were sent back to Mexico during the Great Depression.

When America's thirst for cheap labor was renewed in the 1940s as a result of labor shortages created by World War II, Mexican workers were encouraged to return in large numbers. This time, however, the federal government played a formal, active role in regulating the process. The Bracero program, a guest-worker scheme in place between 1942 and 1964, was created both to assure a cheap source of labor for southwestern agribusiness interests and to inhibit illegal migration. While in effect, it provided more than 4.5 million individual contracts for temporary employment.

The legacy of the Bracero program was the institutionalization of large-scale labor migration from Mexico to the United States. During the decades in which the program existed, an interdependent relationship between employers and migrants became firmly established.[13] Moreover, many "temporary" workers ended up settling in the United States, helping to create the permanent migratory networks that provide a bridge and a base for new arrivals.

An immediate consequence of the Bracero program was that the promise of guaranteed employment unintentionally encouraged illegal border crossings. Large numbers of workers made their way across without going through the formal channels of the recruitment process. As mi-

12. Quoted in Aristide Zolberg and Robert Smith, *Migration Systems in Comparative Perspective: An Analysis of the Inter-American Migration System with Comparative Reference to the Mediterranean-European System* (Washington, D.C.: U.S. Department of State, Bureau of Population, Refugees and Migration, 1996), 9.

13. Kitty Calavita, *Inside the State: The Bracero Program, Immigration and the INS* (New York: Routledge, 1992).

grants streamed north, apprehensions by the Border Patrol jumped from 182,000 in 1947 to more than 850,000 by the end of 1953. In a dramatic effort to impose control, in June 1954 the Eisenhower administration launched Operation Wetback, which resulted in the deportation of hundreds of thousands of Mexicans. Under the command of retired General Joseph Swing, the operation revitalized the Border Patrol and enhanced the sense of order along the boundary.[14]

Yet even as the Border Patrol was engaged in highly publicized mass roundups of illegal migrants, the government was making it easier to import Mexican laborers legally through the Bracero program. Thus, while apprehensions of illegal border crossers dropped sharply in 1955–56, the number of imported Bracero workers rose. In fact, to enhance the appearance of control while also assuring an adequate supply of labor, the Border Patrol often played both enforcer and facilitator. As the immigration scholar Kitty Calavita notes, "Illegal immigrants, or 'wetbacks,' were often 'dried out' by the INS Border Patrol, who escorted them to the Mexican border, had them step to the Mexican side, and brought them back as legal braceros." In some cases, she points out, "the Border Patrol 'paroled' illegal immigrants directly to employers."[15]

Thus, although the Bracero program helped create the appearance of a more orderly, regulated, and temporary labor flow, it also created an increasingly awkward image problem for the state. In 1960 the Eisenhower administration was deeply embarrassed by the CBS documentary *Harvest of Shame,* which drew public attention to the deplorable working conditions of Bracero laborers.[16] It also added legitimacy to labor union pressures to end the guest-worker program.

By formally ending the program a few years later, the administration distanced itself from the appearance of officially sanctioning poor working conditions. All that changed, however, was the legal status of the Mexican workers; they continued to be welcomed by employers who had come to rely on this cheap and flexible labor supply and who had little to fear from the law, since the hiring of illegals was not a felony.[17] By exempting em-

14. The massive sweeps of Operation Wetback would be illegal today, given court decisions that have enhanced the rights of immigrants. It should also be noted that the operation sparked a new form of illegal entry—by means of fraudulent documents such as tourist cards and birth certificates.

15. Kitty Calavita, "U.S. Immigration and Policy Responses: The Limits of Legislation," in *Controlling Immigration: A Global Perspective,* ed. Wayne A. Cornelius, Philip L. Martin, and James Hollifield (Stanford, Calif.: Stanford University Press, 1994), 59.

16. Zolberg and Smith, *Migration Systems,* 14.

17. In 1952, Congress passed an act that made it illegal to "harbor, transport, or conceal illegal entrants." Employment, however, was excluded from the category of "harboring," thanks to an amendment (called the Texas proviso) which was a concession to agribusiness interests. See Calavita, "U.S. Immigration and Policy Responses," 60.

ployers from any responsibility, the complicity of the state in facilitating the importation of Mexican workers continued as before, albeit in a much less public form. Illegal entry rose sharply in the following decades, the formal Bracero system having simply been replaced by an informal one.

The incentives for clandestine entry were further reinforced by the 1965 Immigration Act, which for the first time imposed a limit of 120,000 immigrant visas for the Western Hemisphere. Moreover, the 1976 decision to limit visas to 20,000 per year per individual country in the Western Hemisphere created an enormous backlog of applicants from Mexico— for whom, as the front door of legal entry became more regulated, the backdoor of illegal entry became more attractive.[18]

The illegal nature of the labor flow benefited both employers and the state. For employers, the illegal status of the labor force assured compliance and low wages: lacking public support and state protection, illegal immigrants were less likely to organize or complain about working conditions. For U.S. officials, the very fact that the workers were in the country without a formal invitation helped reduce the appearance of direct government complicity. As long as illegal immigration remained outside the media spotlight, the evasion of U.S. border controls by unauthorized entrants would not become a political embarrassment. For the time being, at least, the clandestine cross-border labor flow was largely off the political map. As a result, its rapid increase in the 1960s and 1970s was not matched by a similar increase in INS enforcement capacity. Interior enforcement was almost nonexistent, and border controls remained at token levels. Even as the number of border apprehensions increased from approximately 71,000 in 1960 to more than a million in 1978, the budget of the Border Patrol remained less than the budget of many city police departments.[19] Minimal political support in Washington meant that the Border Patrol would remain a relatively small force. In few other policy arenas was the gap between official rhetoric and practice more pronounced than in the area of immigration control.

The limited effectiveness of enforcement meant that illegal entry remained a relatively simple and inexpensive activity: migrants either smuggled themselves across the border or hired a local professional, called a *coyote*. The sheer magnitude of the clandestine labor flow, however, heightened competition between smugglers to service it, and with the dispersion of the flow from agricultural to urban areas, smuggling gradually

18. Christian Joppke, "Why Liberal States Accept Unwanted Immigration," *World Politics* 50, no. 2 (1998): 272.

19. The Border Patrol's 1980 budget was less than the budget of the Baltimore police department and less than half that of the Philadelphia police force. Michael Teitelbaum, "Right versus Right: Immigration and Refugee Policy—the United States," *Foreign Affairs* 59, no. 1 (1980): 55.

became better organized. Government reports suggest that smuggling organizations had grown in size and complexity by the mid-1970s. Still, the use of a professional smuggler remained more a convenience than a necessity. In fiscal year (FY) 1970 only 8.4 percent of the illegal migrants caught by the Border Patrol in the southwestern region had attempted entry with a smuggler. This figure rose to 13.5 percent in FY 1975. Apprehension statistics, of course, probably understate the amount of smuggling going on, since migrants who pay a professional are less likely to be apprehended than those who do not. Penalties remained low: less than 50 percent of the smugglers caught between 1973 and 1975 were prosecuted, most on a misdemeanor charge.[20]

The services of a smuggler generally meant a faster and safer trip across the border and could even include door-to-door service from the point of departure in the sending community to the point of destination in places such as Los Angeles. This was particularly useful to first-time border crossers who were unfamiliar with the terrain and the enforcement-evasion game. Hiring a smuggler did involve personal risks (there was potential for theft and physical abuse), but attempting the clandestine border crossing without such help increased the likelihood of assault by border thieves and abuse by the authorities.

Border enforcement, failing to deter illegal crossings significantly, was largely a ritualized performance. The Border Patrol could cover only about 10 percent of the nearly 2,000-mile-long border, and the arrests it did make were more apparent than real.[21] Even though the INS insisted that "prompt apprehension and return to country of origin is a positive deterrent to illegal reentry and related violations," the evidence suggests that migrants simply kept trying to cross until they eventually succeeded.[22] Arrest statistics had little to do with actual deterrence and everything to do with bureaucratic incentives. If little else, high apprehension numbers provided political ammunition in annual budget requests. Indeed, the Border Patrol could boast that it made more arrests than any other law enforcement agency. In the numbers game, then, it could at least show that it was keeping busy. The failure to provide a reasonable measure of effectiveness was even given a positive spin: as a 1973 INS publication put it,

20. See Comptroller General of the United States, *Smugglers, Illicit Documents, and Schemes Are Undermining U.S. Controls over Immigration: Report to the Congress by the Comptroller General of the United States* (Washington, D.C., 30 August 1976), 5–6, 18.

21. Comptroller General of the United States, *Illegal Entry at United States–Mexico Border: Multiagency Enforcement Efforts Have Not Been Effective in Stemming the Flow of Drugs and People; Report to the Congress by the Comptroller General of the United States* (Washington, D.C., 2 December 1977), 7.

22. INS annual report, 1978, cited in Sherrie A. Kossoudji, "Playing Cat and Mouse at the U.S.-Mexican Border," *Demography* 29, no. 2 (1992): 161.

"The Border Patrol's contribution to our country's security and welfare is so far reaching that it cannot be measured"; the patrol "has maintained a reputation for getting the job done."[23]

Both the Border Patrol and the illegal border crossers benefited from an arrest system based on "prompt apprehension and return to country of origin." For the Border Patrol, lack of detention space for a high volume of crossers necessitated a speedy removal process based on "voluntary departure." And for the migrants, a quick return to the Mexican side was welcomed because it shortened the delay before another attempt at crossing.[24] Repeated arrests merely postponed entry but helped Border Patrol agents inflate arrest statistics and improve their internal performance evaluations. External reviewers, however, were less impressed. As one government study bluntly concluded: "Presently the border is a revolving door.... We repatriate undocumented workers on a massive scale.... The illegals cooperate by agreeing to voluntary departure and significant numbers promptly re-enter. It is not unusual for an illegal to undergo multiple apprehensions and re-entries for there are no serious deterrents."[25]

A clandestine form of cross-border interdependence gradually developed as a result of decades of large-scale Mexican migration. On the U.S. side, employers (especially in agriculture but increasingly in other sectors of the economy as well) became accustomed to a cheap, reliable, and disposable labor force. At the same time, Mexico became increasingly reliant on exporting its labor surplus. Remittances from migrant workers provided much-needed foreign exchange (amounting to several billion dollars) which was especially important because it went directly to lower-income households. Entire sending communities became economically dependent on such remittances (which also helped fund the northward trip of other community members), many of which became little more than "nurseries and nursing homes" for community members who were employed in the United States.[26]

The Mexican state itself came to rely on the United States as a safety valve for the nation's unemployment problem. Though not officially promoting illegal migration, government officials took no steps to curb it, and in some respects Mexican policies actually encouraged such migration.

23. Immigration and Naturalization Service, *The Border Patrol: Its Origins and Its Work* (Washington, D.C.: Immigration and Naturalization Service, 1973).

24. Josiah M. Heyman calls this dynamic the "voluntary departure complex"; see his "Putting Power into the Anthropology of Bureaucracy: The Immigration and Naturalization Service at the Mexico–United States Border," *Current Anthropology* 36, no. 2 (1995): 261–87.

25. Domestic Council's Committee on Illegal Aliens, Preliminary Report, December 1976, quoted in Comptroller General of the United States, *Illegal Entry at United States–Mexico Border*, 17.

26. Wayne Cornelius, quoted in Zolberg and Smith, *Migration Systems*, 34.

The state-promoted development model generated economic growth—but without significant gains in employment. Economic policies that created what Philip Martin calls "growth without jobs" indirectly encouraged workers to turn to the underground exit option of migrating to the United States.[27] In rural communities that option was reinforced by the fact that Mexican economic and social policies had a strong urban bias.[28]

Increasingly, the exit option included work not only in U.S. agriculture (traditionally the backbone of unauthorized employment) but also in urban-based sectors of the economy such as services and construction. Not surprisingly, as employment opportunities expanded spatially and occupationally, migration became more permanent, less seasonal, and more city-focused—and thus increasingly visible to the general public. The problem, of course, was that although their illegal status was part of what made Mexican workers attractive to employers, this status reinforced public hostility. And as their numbers grew, expanding beyond the traditional confines of rural agricultural regions in the West, public tolerance gradually deteriorated.

These changes helped to further politicize the issue of illegal immigration in the late 1970s and early 1980s. Years of U.S. congressional debate over how to respond to illegal immigration culminated in 1986 with the passage of the Immigration Reform and Control Act (IRCA). IRCA introduced employer sanctions for the first time, authorized an expansion of the Border Patrol, and offered a general legalization program (as well as a special legalization program for agricultural workers). Some two million Mexicans were eventually given legal status—far more than initially projected. The proponents of IRCA argued that this supply of newly legalized workers would saturate the domestic demand for immigrant labor, while sanctions against employers would deter the hiring of illegal workers. This combination, it was hoped, would inhibit future unauthorized migration.

In practice, however, IRCA generated perverse and unintended (though not unpredictable) consequences that contributed to the very problem for which the law was sold as a remedy. For example, many onetime immigrants who had gone back to Mexico returned to claim legalization papers. And those who were legalized under IRCA helped facilitate the arrival of new illegal immigrants. Meanwhile, the employer sanctions proved to be largely symbolic; their immediate impact was to spark an enormous underground business in fraudulent documents. Since the new law did not require employers to verify the authenticity of the documents, they still

27. Philip Martin, cited in ibid., 21.

28. See Bryan Roberts and Agustin Escobar Latapi, "Mexican Social and Economic Policy and Emigration," in *At the Crossroads: Mexican Migration and U.S. Policy,* ed. Frank D. Bean, Rodolfo O. De la Garza, Bryan Roberts, and Sidney Weintraub (Lanham, Md.: Rowman & Littlefield, 1997).

risked little by hiring illegal workers. And fraudulent papers, though a necessity for migrants, were relatively inexpensive and easy to obtain. Any of some twenty-nine different documents could be used to satisfy the document-check requirement.

As a result, illegal workers and their employers had little trouble adapting to the new rules of the immigration enforcement game. The only real change was the necessity of maintaining at least the appearance of hiring legal labor. INS inspectors were satisfied as long as employers made sure to go through the ritual of asking for documents and filling out the proper paperwork; employers could be prosecuted only if it could be proved that they "knowingly" hired illegal workers. The perceived increase in employer "compliance," in turn, helped the INS improve its own enforcement image.

Another key image effect of IRCA was the appearance of a more controlled border—at least in the short term. Border apprehensions from FY 1986 to 1989 dropped by nearly half, from more than 1.6 million to fewer than 855,000. The eventual legalization of some 2 million Mexicans in the United States (many of whom had previously been going back and forth illegally) contributed to this image of enhanced control. But starting in 1989, apprehensions again began to rise sharply and by the early 1990s had returned to their pre-IRCA levels. Not only were the employer sanctions proving to have little deterrent effect, but the millions of migrants legalized under IRCA were able to provide a stronger and more stable base for unauthorized arrivals. One U.S. government commission even concluded that the legalization programs for agricultural workers had unintentionally promoted more immigration by sending the message that being illegally employed in farm work in the United States would facilitate becoming a legal immigrant.[29]

Thus, in the end, IRCA became part of the problem rather than the solution. The immediate political benefit of the law for its proponents was to defuse domestic pressure by finally "doing something" about illegal immigration. Yet it helped set the stage for the intense anti-immigrant backlash in the early 1990s—with the southwestern border becoming a focal point of media scrutiny, political debate, and public outrage.

Drug Smuggling

The entry of drugs into the mix of smuggling activities in the first decades of the twentieth century profoundly transformed the dynamics of

29. Commission on Agricultural Workers, *Report of the Commission on Agricultural Workers* (Washington D.C., 1993).

law enforcement and law evasion across the U.S.-Mexico border. U.S. prohibition laws, beginning with the 1909 Opium Exclusion Act and the 1914 Harrison Narcotics Law, provided a major boost for Mexico's nascent drug export sector.[30] Marijuana had been grown in Mexico since the nineteenth century, and in the first decades of the twentieth century Chinese immigrants brought opium growing to the states of Sinaloa and Sonora.

The new U.S. prohibitions and the subsequent rise in drug smuggling created political problems for the central government in Mexico, which exercised only minimal control over its northern border states. Not only did the prohibitions generate concerns about incursions into Mexican territory by American law enforcers and drug smugglers, but the emerging Mexican drug trade was located in border states that were areas of antigovernment opposition. The clandestine border economy (of which drugs had now become a part) provided a financial base for strongmen such as Estéban Cantú, who ruled Baja California as his own private fiefdom from 1914 to 1920.[31]

U.S. antidrug laws were eventually matched by similar laws on the Mexican side of the border. In 1916 Mexico prohibited opium imports; in 1923 it banned the importation of all narcotics. In 1927 a Mexican decree outlawed the export of heroin and marijuana. This was done partly to pacify the United States and conform to an emerging international drug prohibition regime. But the criminalization of drugs in Mexico also reflected state efforts to gain greater control over the border and to limit further U.S. territorial incursions.[32] In practice, however, enforcement of drug laws was minimal. Moreover, during World War II the United States actually encouraged Mexican opium production (for morphine) and marijuana production (hemp for rope) as part of the war effort.

In the 1950s and 1960s Mexico supplied about 75 percent of the U.S. marijuana market and 10–15 percent of the heroin market. In the early 1970s Mexico's share of the U.S. heroin market rose sharply, not simply as a result of high U.S. consumer demand but because of law enforcement initiatives on the other side of the globe. Turkey had been the primary supplier to the booming U.S. heroin market in the 1960s, but when the Turkish government (under intense U.S. pressure) prohibited opium production and implemented a strict control program in 1972, production shifted to a logical and much closer alternative: Mexico. Thus, the unintentional feedback effect of targeting Turkey (and severing its "French

30. Drug prohibition became institutionalized at the international level with the 1909 Shanghai Convention and the Hague Opium Convention of 1911–12. A drug prohibition regime was expanded through the United Nations in the post–World War II period.

31. See María Celia Toro, *Mexico's "War" on Drugs: Causes and Consequences* (Boulder, Colo.: Lynne Rienner, 1995).

32. Ibid., 67.

Connection" with Marseilles) was to transplant the heroin supply problem to Mexico.

As part of the Nixon administration's declaration of a "war on drugs" (the first use of the term), Operation Intercept was launched in September 1969. Through intensive scrutiny of vehicles crossing the southwestern border, the highly publicized operation predictably created enormous traffic jams and jolted the local economies of border cities. The Mexican tourist and fresh produce industries were especially hurt. Minimal amounts of drugs were seized in "the nation's largest peacetime search and seizure operation by civil authorities." Yet the primary purpose of the operation was not to deter drugs at the border but to signal Richard Nixon's displeasure with Mexico's own drug eradication effort.[33] Loud protests by the Mexican government and the economic stress on border cities led U.S. officials to relax their pressure on the ports of entry—but not until Mexico had promised a more aggressive antidrug program.

Operation Intercept significantly elevated the drug issue on the U.S.-Mexico policy agenda and ushered in a new era in cross-border drug control initiatives. The centerpiece was Mexico's launching of Operation Condor in 1975, the most ambitious eradication effort ever undertaken by any country. The northern states of Sinaloa, Durango, and Chihuahua were especially targeted. The results were dramatic: Mexico's share of the U.S. marijuana market fell from over 75 percent in 1976 to as low as 4 percent in 1981, and its share of the U.S. heroin market plummeted from 67 percent in 1976 to 25 percent in 1980. These reductions were primarily accomplished through the use of herbicides in aerial eradication, as well as the deployment of military troops for manual eradication. Cross-border law enforcement collaboration between the United States and Mexico, including intelligence sharing, surveillance, and training, also contributed to the campaign's impressive outcome.[34]

The operation generated significant rewards for officials on both sides of the border. For Washington, it demonstrated the viability of a supply-reduction strategy based on bilateral cooperation, intensified law enforcement at the source of production, and greater use of technology; indeed, it was considered a model program for all drug source countries. At the same time, the operation had the added advantage of providing much greater U.S. law enforcement access to Mexican territory and police forces. Richard Craig notes that the Mexican Attorney General's Office had obtained from the United States an air wing that was bigger and better than most air forces in Latin America. For the military, the operation provided

33. Richard B. Craig, "Operation Intercept: The International Politics of Pressure," *Review of Politics* 42, no. 4 (1980): 564.

34. Toro, *Mexico's "War" on Drugs*, 27.

a means to gain training that conveniently resembled counterinsurgency tactics; government authority was reimposed in many rural areas. Meanwhile, Mexican leaders were pleased that their operation projected a positive international image.[35]

It was less noticed, however, that the very success of the eradication effort led to a restructuring rather than a permanent reduction of Mexico's role in the drug trade. Thanks to the antidrug offensive, the least efficient and competitive smuggling groups were weeded out (jailed or forced out of business), leaving the market open for sophisticated organizations that relied more heavily on violence, corruption, and intimidation. Indeed, some of Mexico's leading smuggling organizations (not only for drugs but for other commodities as well) emerged during the height of the government's antidrug offensive.[36] As one Mexican analyst has argued, "The impact of the U.S.-inspired eradication program on the market place has been . . . to give comparative advantage to large scale criminal organizations."[37]

Meanwhile, part of the collateral damage of the antidrug offensive was more extensive corruption within Mexican law enforcement. Increased drug control brought with it increased proximity of the police to drug trafficking—and an increased incentive for traffickers to bribe them. This relationship, in turn, retarded the much-needed professionalization of the federal police forces.[38] The spread of corruption also made it increasingly difficult to sustain the success of the drug control campaign. And unfortunately for the Mexican government, a byproduct of the campaign's impressive early accomplishments was an inflated U.S. expectation of success.

Within a few years, the Mexican drug trade had adjusted to the new enforcement environment. Not only did production of marijuana and opium poppy again rapidly expand (this time in more dispersed and less visible plots), but by the mid-1980s Mexico was becoming an increasingly important transshipment point for South American cocaine bound for the U.S. market. The full significance of this change and its impact on the southwestern border region would not be recognized until years later.

Drug trafficking and drug enforcement grew together in the 1980s.

35. See Richard B. Craig, "U.S. Narcotics Policy towards Mexico: Consequences for the Bilateral Relationship," in *The Drug Connection in U.S.-Mexican Relations,* ed. Guadalupe González and Marta Tienda (La Jolla: Center for U.S.-Mexican Studies, University of California at San Diego, 1989), 75.

36. Reuter and Ronfeldt, *Quest for Integrity,* 13.

37. Samuel Del Villar, "The Illicit U.S.-Mexico Drug Market: Failure of Policy and an Alternative," in *Mexico and the United States: Managing the Relationship,* ed. Riordan Roett (Boulder, Colo.: Westview, 1988), 22.

38. Miguél Ruiz-Cabañas, cited in Reuter and Ronfeldt, *Quest for Integrity,* 16.

Beginning with the Reagan administration's launching of a new "war on drugs," the U.S. campaign for control escalated at home and abroad. Budgets grew, agency missions expanded, tougher laws were introduced, and the overall importance of the issue on the policy agenda was significantly elevated. At the time, however, the focus was not on the U.S.-Mexico border but on the influx of Colombian cocaine and marijuana through south Florida. The South Florida Task Force, under the direction of Vice President George Bush, was launched in January 1982 to target air and sea smuggling routes in the Southeast (it would later serve as a model for anti-drug efforts in the Southwest).

The interdiction campaign for the first time included recruiting the U.S. military to play a support role for the Coast Guard and the Customs Service. Turning to the military for assistance required loosening the 1878 Posse Comitatus Act (prohibiting military involvement in domestic law enforcement), which in turn would open the door for an enhanced military role on the southwestern border in later years. Funding for the Defense Department's interdiction campaign increased from $4.9 million in FY 1982 to an estimated $387 million in FY 1987.[39] Contributing to the growing fusion between military and law enforcement missions was President Ronald Reagan's 1986 security directive which for the first time officially classified drugs as a national security threat.

Funding for interdiction doubled between 1982 and 1987 and continued to focus most intensively on the Southeast. Federal cocaine seizures rose sharply as well, from two tons in 1981 to twenty-seven tons in 1986 to one hundred tons in 1989.[40] But these seizures, though statistically impressive, did little to reduce the drug flow; in fact, cocaine imports more than doubled between 1984 and 1986.[41] U.S. officials pointed to the record amounts of drugs they were seizing as an indicator of policy progress, but part of the reason they were seizing more was that more drugs were flowing across the border.[42]

Even though pouring more resources into an increasingly militarized interdiction campaign made little sense from the standpoint of a cost-benefit calculus of deterrence, it made a great deal of sense in a political calculus of image projection. With Democrats and Republicans out-toughing each other over the drug issue, pushing for a bigger and better border interdiction effort became a favorite means of displaying political resolve. In fact,

39. John Moore, "No Quick Fix," *National Journal* 19 (21 November 1987): 2955.
40. Toro, *Mexico's "War" on Drugs,* 31.
41. Moore, "No Quick Fix," 2956.
42. "The limited seizure and trafficking data available indicate seizures increasing as smuggling increases": Congress, Office of Technology Assessment, *The Border War on Drugs* (Washington, D.C., March 1987), 51.

in 1988, the House of Representatives voted 385 to 23 to amend the defense bill by ordering the deployment of the U.S. military within forty-five days of enactment to "substantially halt the unlawful penetration of U.S. borders by aircraft and vessels carrying narcotics"—even though the Pentagon made it clear that such a demand was unrealistic.[43] Commenting on the Senate's effort to increase the interdiction role of the military in 1988, Senator John McCain (R-Ariz.) spoke for many in Congress: "This is such an emotional issue—I mean, we're at war here—that voting no would be too difficult to explain." Voting against it, he said, would be "voting against the war on drugs. Nobody wants to do that."[44] Reflecting on the debate over a 1988 drug bill, Representative Charles Schumer (D-N.Y.) said, "It's quick-hit, image over substance, and nobody cares if it's going to work."[45]

Out-toughing occurred on the campaign trail as well. The 1986 race between Florida's Republican Senator Paula Hawkins and Democratic Governor Bob Graham was one example. When Senator Hawkins described herself as "the general in the Senate's war on drugs," the governor countered with a television advertisement. In it he was shown first in a police helicopter, giving a tough line on drug control, and then next to a captured smugglers' airplane, calling for more military involvement in the drug war and attacking Hawkins for voting against increased funding for the Coast Guard's drug war effort. The *Congressional Quarterly* described the election-driven escalation: "In the closing weeks of the Congressional election season, taking the pledge becomes a familiar feature of campaign life. Thirty years ago, candidates pledged to battle domestic communism. . . . In 1986, the pledge issue is drugs."[46]

The Maginot Line–style strategy in south Florida did not significantly deter drug importations, but it did powerfully influence the location, methods, and organization of drug smuggling. Its most important impact was to push much of the traffic to the Southwest, making Colombian traffickers increasingly reliant on Mexican smuggling networks, as some in the Drug Enforcement Administration (DEA) recognized. Testifying at a Foreign Affairs Committee task force hearing on 7 October 1987, assistant DEA administrator David Westrate noted that the enforcement crackdown in the Southeast had redirected more cocaine shipments through Mexico:

> Now that's got a serious downside, other than it opens a second major theater for us to address, which is the southwest border. . . . It also has produced a

43. *Congressional Quarterly Almanac* 44 (1989): 85–111.
44. Quoted in *Washington Post,* 15 June 1988.
45. Quoted in *Washington Post,* 19 September 1988.
46. See "Four Key Issues Playing Role in Congressional Contests," *Congressional Quarterly,* 18 October 1986, 2599.

strong linkage between the Colombian major drug organizations and Mexican drug organizations—a connection we did not have before. And I think that clearly is something that's going to cause us fits in the next couple of years.[47]

In other words, the main impact of the U.S. interdiction strategy was to create more business for Mexican smuggling organizations and more work for law enforcement.

Signaling the growing law enforcement focus on the Southwest, Operation Alliance was launched in June 1986 to coordinate all interdiction efforts along the U.S.-Mexico border (including coordination between the military and civilian agencies).[48] Through Operation Alliance, the increased attention on the Southwest helped fuel the growth of such agencies as the Customs Service.[49] Apparently, the main lesson learned from the experience in the Southeast was the need to replicate the strategy in the Southwest. Coast Guard Admiral Paul Yost testified: "The more money that you spend on it, the more success you are going to have in the interdiction area. . . . We did that in the Caribbean for the last two years, and I'm sure that what we're about to do on the southwest border will also be extremely successful. It is also going to be extremely expensive, and the success expense ratio is going to be a very direct one."[50]

Measuring such success, however, was politically tricky. At a 1987 Senate hearing held in Nogales, Arizona, senator Pete Domenici (R-N.Mex.) summarized the situation:

> Now, I understand that we're shooting at floating targets. I mean, you do well in the Southeast and they [the traffickers] move to the Southwest. We'll load up the Southwest and what happens next? Nonetheless, we have to continue the war on drugs. And for us to sustain the resources, you have to have a few field victories of significant size that are measurable. We have to take that to

47. Quoted in Moore, "No Quick Fix," 2957.

48. According to Alan Eliason, senior tactical coordinator, Operation Alliance was "designed to be a permanent hardening of the nation's drug enforcement posture all along our southwest border": Senate Subcommittee on Treasury, Postal Service, and General Government, Committee on Appropriations, *Southwest Border Law Enforcement and Trade: Hearings,* 100th Cong., 1st sess., 19 August 1987, 260–61.

49. As Customs Commissioner William Von Raab testified (ibid., 24), "The Congress has been very generous and we have responded accordingly. The Customs Service has gone up from 12,000 to 16,000 men and women over the past four years or so. That's quite a strain on an organization. We are going to deploy 250 million dollars' worth of assets across the Southwest border; that's a tough job. We're working closely with the Defense Department in doing that."

50. Testimony of Admiral Paul Yost, U.S. Coast Guard, before the House Select Committee on Narcotics Abuse and Control, *U.S. Narcotics Control Efforts in Mexico and on the Southwest Border,* 99th Cong., 2d sess., 22 July 1986, 34.

the floor and to the committee and tell them we put a billion seven more and it's doing something. And it can't only be measured by manpower, it has to be measured in results.[51]

The reply by Customs Commissioner William Von Raab was predictable: "We're just about 1 year into Operation Alliance. The seizures, which are your typical measure of success, are impressive. Operation Alliance totals 250,000 pounds of marijuana and about 16,000 pounds of cocaine; that's very good." The commissioner further asserted that, based on seizure levels, interdiction had improved ten times in the previous five years. He also noted that air interdiction in the Southwest was being enhanced through the use of airborne warning and control system (AWACS) planes and the deployment of new aerostat radar balloons.[52] Pleased to hear that some progress was being made in controlling the border, none of the committee members questioned what these measures of success actually measured.

At the same hearing, Von Raab acknowledged that "there is good news and bad news" in increased drug seizures: "The good news is that we are catching more drugs because we are getting better at doing our jobs. We have more resources. The bad news is that we are catching more because more is coming across." He concluded that "we are winning the battles, but I am not sure we are winning the war. . . . However, I am extremely comfortable with our performance."[53]

Meanwhile, the business community along the southwestern border was becoming increasingly concerned that intensified drug checks at the official ports of entry, which caused border congestion and traffic jams, were slowing the rise in legal commerce. Thus, not only law enforcement advocates but also the private sector pushed for more federal funding to ugrade the ports of entry. As the president of one brokerage firm told a congressional committee, "The significant increases in commercial and civilian traffic coupled with the need to address the drug problem are creating a disastrous situation for manufacturers, importers, and border city retailers." He warned: "If U.S. Customs is going to service the needs of the commercial sector and civilian sectors and at the same time increase their surveillance and interdiction program for drugs, international trade and relations are going to suffer irreparable harm unless the appropriations for improved facilities and manpower are provided."[54]

51. See Senate Subcommittee, *Southwest Border Law Enforcement and Trade,* 19 August 1987, 25.
52. Ibid., 25, 191, 200.
53. Ibid., 191, 202.
54. Statement of Russell L. Jones, president of Richard L. Jones Customhouse Brokers, before Senate Subcommittee of the Committee on Appropriations, *Southwest Border Law Enforcement and Trade,* 100th Cong., 1st sess., 19 August 1987, 143–44.

Such concerns reflected the dilemma that U.S. officials had partly created for themselves: they had transplanted much of the cocaine trafficking from south Florida to the U.S.-Mexican border, but efforts to harden the border against the illegal trade came into direct conflict with the policy goal of facilitating the expansion of legal trade. In an effort to reconcile these goals, in February 1987 the Customs Service initiated the Southwest Border Strategy, "a seven point action plan designed to improve our ability to facilitate cargo at the border while at the same time increasing our ability to prohibit . . . commercial cargo, trucks and rail cars from being used to conceal narcotics." The most important part of the plan was the implementation of a system called Line Release, which allowed the preapproval of some trucks and the processing of "routine, repetitive shipments in a minute or two."[55] Although it generated little political attention and concern at the time, this system would in later years invite sharp political allegations that drug control was being sacrificed to free trade. Thus, rather than helping to resolve the tension between enforcement and facilitation, Line-Release processing would draw attention to it.

A dramatic sign that the Mexican drug trade had not only recovered from the crackdown of the 1970s but had been transformed into a more violent and corrupting enterprise was the 1985 murder of DEA agent Kiki Camarena in Guadalajara. The murder also demonstrated that the increased capacity of the DEA to pressure Mexican traffickers within Mexico directly (a result of the collaborative enforcement efforts in the 1970s) had brought with it significant new risks. The Camarena affair sent U.S.-Mexican relations into a tailspin, reversing the climate of antidrug cooperation that had been cultivated during the previous decade.

The most visible and immediate U.S. response to Camarena's disappearance was Operation Intercept II in February 1985, involving intensive checks on traffic entering from Mexico and even a partial closing of the border. Similar to its predecessor, Operation Intercept in 1969, the 1985 version had little impact on drug flows but created enormous traffic delays along the border. Its primary purpose, however, was not interdiction but communication: it was intended to display U.S. anger and frustration and to send a strong message to Mexico City. Thus, in 1985 as in 1969, the United States strategically used the border as a high-profile stage from which to signal disapproval of Mexico's antidrug performance.

The diplomatic crisis worsened in 1986. In January, Mexicans were shocked by the DEA-orchestrated kidnapping of René Verdugo Urquídez to the United States to stand trial for his alleged role in Camarena's murder. And on 8 March most of the customs houses on the border were temporarily shut down (the official reason given was the need to search for

55. Testimony of James C. Piatt, U.S. Customs Service, ibid., 306–8.

weapons and drugs being smuggled into the United States by Libyan terrorists). The outspoken Von Raab even publicly accused the governor of Sonora of cultivating opium and marijuana on his own farms and having the farms guarded by the Mexican military.[56]

Heated congressional hearings on the Camarena affair became a public platform for a much broader interrogation of official corruption in Mexico. Regardless of whether the corruption accusations were valid or not, what most offended the Mexicans was the public nature of the Mexico-bashing by U.S. politicians and law enforcement officials. For the first time, the U.S.-Mexico war on drugs also became a full-blown cross-border war of words. Although the entrenchment of drug-related corruption in Mexico had long been well known, it was not until the killing of Camarena that U.S. officials publicly pointed fingers at specific individuals within the Mexican political system and security apparatus. Growing alarm over drug-related corruption in Mexico fueled more general anxiety over the security of the border. The House Select Committee on Narcotics Abuse and Control sponsored a series of hearings in the Southwest and concluded in its final report that the border was "totally out of control and threatening, not only to the region itself, but to the entire country."[57]

The Camarena affair helped spark policy initiatives on both sides of the border that would have long-lasting consequences. In Washington, Camarena's murder provided an important impetus for the U.S. Congress to mandate, as part of the sweeping Anti-Drug Abuse Act of 1986, that the United States make foreign economic and military assistance, votes in multilateral lending institutions, and trade preferences contingent on "full cooperation" with U.S. antidrug objectives. The law created a certification process that required the State Department to publish an annual report on the drug control efforts of source countries; those countries viewed as not sufficiently cooperative could be "decertified." Such an evaluation mechanism would reshape the politics of drug control: the annual review process assured that the antidrug performance of source countries such as Mexico would remain elevated on the U.S. policy agenda and receive substantial media attention. Moreover, once established, this oversight process would be extraordinarily difficult to reverse or modify. Despite widespread criticism of the certification law, policymakers shied away from changing it for fear of appearing "soft on drugs."

In Mexico, meanwhile, investigations into Camarena's death embar-

---

56. Jorge Chabat, "Drug Trafficking in U.S.-Mexican Relations: What You See Is What You Get," in *Drug Trafficking in the Americas*, ed. Bruce M. Bagley and William O. Walker III (Coral Gables, Fla.: North South Center, University of Miami, 1994), 378.

57. House Select Committee on Narcotics Abuse and Control, *Southwest Border Hearings (El Paso, Texas, Tucson, Arizona, San Diego, California) and Mexico Trip Report (Nogales, Mexico City, Culiacan)*, 99th Cong., 2d sess., 12–19 January 1986, 3.

rassed the government by exposing close links between traffickers and the security apparatus. Largely because of pressure from Washington, the notoriously corrupt Federal Security Directorate (which had long enjoyed close ties to the U.S. Central Intelligence Agency) was quickly disbanded. Also, Rafaél Caro Quintéro, the trafficker accused of being responsible for Camarena's murder, was arrested in April 1985. It is "a sad irony," noted a 1986 U.S. congressional report, that Camarena's murder "has ultimately benefited U.S. drug control efforts in Mexico. The American outrage over this incident has brought Mexican cooperation in many levels of narcotics control, as well as some dismissals of corrupt individuals."[58]

Partly to signal its renewed commitment to fighting drugs, the Mexican government continued to devote more resources to enforcement. For example, the percentage of the attorney general's budget devoted to drug control rose from 32.5 percent in 1985 to more than 60 percent in 1988. At the same time, the government continued to expand the role of the military in crop eradication. In 1987 this activity involved some 25,000 soldiers—up from only 5,000 in the late 1970s.[59] The increased militarization of the antidrug effort was legitimated by the declaration by President Miguél De La Madrid Hurtado that drug trafficking was a national security threat (paralleling a similar declaration by his U.S. counterpart). Given that the language of national security had been rare in Mexican political discourse, his statement represented a major departure from the past.

These changes, however, were merely a prelude to the sweeping antidrug initiatives by the administration of Carlos Salinas de Gortari. The challenge facing the new Mexican president was to overcome the poisonous fallout from the Camarena affair in order to nurture a closer economic relationship with the United States. Success in doing so depended at least partly on projecting a new image of Mexico's drug control effort and taming American anxiety over the flow of drugs across the border. Fortunately for Salinas, he had key allies on the U.S. side, reflected in the celebrated "spirit of Houston" that emerged from the November 1988 meeting between the recently elected Presidents Bush and Salinas.

But even as Salinas and Bush began to orchestrate a metamorphosis of the U.S.-Mexico economic relationship, its clandestine underside was rapidly changing as well. Official estimates suggest that Mexican marijuana and heroin exports alone were already generating $2.2 to $6.8 billion by the late 1980s, making drugs a sizable export industry.[60] And the height-

58. Ibid., 17.
59. María Celia Toro, "Drug Trafficking from a National Security Perspective," in *Mexico: In Search of Security,* ed. Bruce M. Bagley and Sergio Aguayo Quezada (Coral Gables, Fla.: North South Center, University of Miami, 1993), 326.
60. Cited in Reuter and Ronfeldt, *Quest for Integrity,* 7.

ened role of cocaine in Mexican drug smuggling was dramatically elevating the financial stakes of the trade.

As the clandestine side of the U.S.-Mexico economic relationship evolved and developed over time, the flow of drugs and migrant labor became its most prominent and controversial components. State practices on both sides of the border played an essential role (often unintended) in creating and transforming this underground cross-border economy and helped set the stage for the rapid expansion of immigration and drug controls in recent years. Clandestine economic flows had been a constant in the history of the U.S.-Mexico border, yet for the most part commanded only sporadic policy attention. Border policing remained a peripheral and low-profile activity, and smuggling rarely attracted the national political spotlight. This situation began to change significantly in the 1970s and 1980s—but even the policy initiatives of those decades were entirely overshadowed by the rapid escalation of policing in the 1990s.

CHAPTER FOUR

The Escalation of Drug Control

The 1990s saw an unprecedented escalation of U.S. and Mexican efforts to curb the smuggling of drugs across their shared border.[1] While failing to deter the drug flow, enforcement initiatives generated highly visible and symbolically appealing operational results that projected an image of a shared cross-border commitment to drug control. Such image projection was an essential political ingredient for creating and sustaining a new and more intimate cross-border economic relationship. In other words, the building of more police barriers was intimately connected to the dismantling of economic barriers between the two countries. The persistent failings and perverse and unintended consequences of the antidrug campaign, however, made managing the border and bilateral relations over the drug issue increasingly awkward and difficult in the post-NAFTA era. And these problems, in turn, reinforced the pressures to escalate.

PUSHING COCAINE SMUGGLING TO THE U.S.-MEXICO BORDER

As long as the heroin and marijuana that traditionally dominated the business of drug smuggling across the southwestern border were produced

1. On the U.S. side, federal antidrug funding for the southwestern border reached about $1.7 billion in FY 1997 (supporting more than 7,700 agents and inspectors) and has continued to grow: between FY 1993 and 1997, Customs Service funding for the southwestern border grew 72 percent; from FY 1990 through 1997, DEA funding for the southwest border area rose 55 percent (and a further 24 percent in FY 1998), and the INS antidrug budget rose 164 percent; and between FY 1991 and 1997, the Defense Department's counternarcotics support increased 53 percent. See Office of National Drug Control Policy, *Briefing Book: An Overview of Federal Drug Control Programs on the Southwest Border* (Washington, D.C., August 1997).

within Mexico, Mexican drug smuggling remained primarily a local and regionally based activity. In the mid-1980s, however, a strategic alliance began to emerge between Colombian cocaine exporters and Mexico's smuggling organizations. Intensified U.S. pressure on trafficking routes through the Caribbean and south Florida, beginning in the early 1980s, created incentives for Colombian traffickers to turn to their Mexican counterparts. The percentage of cocaine entering the United States through Mexico had been negligible in the early 1980s. But according to State Department estimates, by 1989 nearly a third of cocaine exports were routed through Mexican territory; by 1992, more than half; in later years, as high as 75–80 percent.[2]

In short, although the antidrug campaign in the Southeast helped U.S. lawmakers and law enforcers show immediate and visible interdiction results during a period of rising domestic anxiety about drugs, its impact on smuggling patterns was to relocate the problem to the southwestern border and fuel a booming business for Mexican smugglers. Focused narrowly on their assigned task of deterring drugs in the southeast, U.S. antidrug strategists apparently paid little attention to what the repercussions would be for Mexico, the border region, and U.S.-Mexican relations.[3]

The U.S. interdiction crackdown in the 1980s disrupted not only the traditional routes for cocaine smuggling, through the Caribbean and south Florida, but also the favored method of such smuggling: light aircraft. Extending the U.S. radar net from the Southeast to the Southwest forced much of the trade out of the air. The United States had constructed what one senior customs official described as a "Maginot line of radar" across the border that reduced air smuggling by an estimated 75 percent from 1982 levels.[4]

In the process, the Customs Service built up an air interdiction infrastructure. Between 1986 and 1992 it tripled the size of its air fleet and increased its air program personnel sixfold. A majority of Department of Defense (DOD) interdiction resources also targeted air smuggling.[5] As one observer put it, "Unused DOD resources looking for a mission have mar-

2. State Department estimates cited in Peter H. Smith, "Semiorganized International Crime: Drug Trafficking in Mexico," in *Transnational Crime in the Americas*, ed. Tom Farer (New York: Routledge, 1999), 195.

3. Author interview with former Joint Task Force Six official, San Diego, Calif., 21 February 1997.

4. Congressional Research Service, *Drug Interdiction: U.S. Programs, Policy, and Options for Congress*, report prepared by the Senate Caucus on International Narcotics Control, September 1996, proceedings of a seminar held by the Congressional Research Service, 12 December 1995, 19–20.

5. *Houston Chronicle*, 16 August 1992.

ried the ambition of the Customs Service to have its own air forces."[6] Some 40 percent of AWACS airtime was devoted to drug surveillance in 1990.[7] And even the North American Air Defense Command (NORAD), once focused on detecting Soviet missiles, redirected some of its energies toward detecting drug-smuggling aircraft.

U.S. officials boasted that the sharp drop in air smuggling displayed the effectiveness of interdiction.[8] But the actual effect was to redirect rather than reduce the drug flow.[9] With much of the traffic pushed out of the air, road transportation networks through Mexico to the U.S. market became an integral component of the cocaine trade. The Mexican organizations that controlled smuggling along these routes were more than willing to sell their services—off-loading, storing, and smuggling—to Colombia's cocaine exporters.

ESCALATION DURING THE SALINAS YEARS

When Carlos Salinas assumed the Mexican presidency in December 1988, he faced the daunting twin tasks of coping with a more powerful, internationally connected Mexican drug-smuggling business (largely thanks to the "success" of U.S. law enforcement in the Caribbean and south Florida) and with rising U.S. political expectations that Mexico demonstrate much greater commitment to doing something about it. It was critical to his broader agenda—sweeping market reforms at home and deeper economic integration with the United States—that the drug issue be effectively managed in order not to undermine the process. His counterparts in the Bush and, later, the Clinton administration shared this objective. While pushing Mexico to adopt an aggressive antidrug campaign, they also collaborated with Mexico in selling the campaign's results to the U.S. Congress and the media.

6. Testimony of Jack Blum, former Senate investigator, Senate Subcommittee of the Committee on Appropriations, *Border Drug Interdiction*, 103d Cong., 1st sess., 24 February 1993, 85.

7. *Los Angeles Times*, 9 April 1990.

8. Testimony of Michael Lane, acting customs commissioner, Senate Subcommittee of the Committee on Appropriations, *Border Drug Interdiction*, 103d Cong., 1st sess., 24 February 1993, 5. "Interdiction is a successful and proven concept," he said, pointing to a three-quarter drop in air smuggling.

9. According to the General Accounting Office, "interdiction has not made a difference in terms of the hard goals of deterring smugglers and reducing the flow of cocaine": testimony of Louis J. Rodrigues, Senate Subcommittee on Treasury, Postal Service, and General Government, Committee on Appropriations, *Border Drug Interdiction*, 103d Cong., 1st sess., 25 February 1993, 147.

Eleven days after taking office, Salinas assured a visiting U.S. congressional delegation that he would "make life miserable for drug traffickers." Representative Charles Rangel (D-N.Y.), who was part of the delegation and who had previously been critical of Mexican antidrug efforts, noted, "We were not so arrogant as to ask for specifics, but we were indeed overwhelmed by the specifics that were given to us, and more importantly by the depth of that commitment."[10] Indeed, Salinas did launch an aggressive campaign to revitalize the Mexican antidrug program, declaring that drug trafficking was the number one security threat facing the nation.

Signaling a new willingness to work with the United States, in 1989 Mexico signed a comprehensive agreement on bilateral cooperation and in 1991 endorsed the Treaty on Cooperation for Mutual Legal Assistance. These accords, in turn, created various bilateral interagency groups for coordinating the antidrug effort. Reflecting the heightened importance of the drug issue on the bilateral agenda, a new section within the Mexican Ministry of Foreign Affairs was established to handle matters related to drug and arms trafficking, and drug policy specialists were added to the Mexican embassy and consulates in the United States.[11] Meanwhile, to bolster Mexico's international image, in 1990 the Mexican government became party to the 1988 United Nations Convention against Trafficking in Illicit Narcotics and Dangerous Drugs.

Among his efforts to build a more formidable drug control apparatus, Salinas created a national security council, developed a new intelligence agency, set up a unit within the attorney general's office for drug enforcement, and organized new antidrug units of the federal judicial police for rapid interdiction.[12] In 1992 the Planning Center for Drug Control (CENDRO) was established to improve interagency coordination and intelligence gathering. And in 1993 the National Institute to Combat Drugs (modeled after the DEA) became the lead agency for antidrug planning and supervision.

The buildup of Mexico's antidrug program was particularly impressive, given that it occurred during a time of deep cuts in overall government spending. Indeed, in an era defined by massive deregulation and privatization, drug control stood out as one of the few areas where state intervention in the economy was increasing. The resources devoted to drug control by the Mexican Attorney General's Office tripled from the late 1980s to the early 1990s. Drug control came to dominate the Mexican criminal justice system: the majority of the federal budget for the administration of

10. Quoted in *New York Times*, 12 December 1988.
11. Peter Reuter and David Ronfeldt, *Quest for Integrity: The Mexican-U.S. Drug Issue in the 1980s* (Santa Monica, Calif.: RAND Corporation, 1991).
12. Ibid.

justice was being applied to the effort by the end of the 1980s. The "Mexican attorney general's office," one Mexican scholar has observed, "has basically become an antidrug law enforcement agency."[13] To give the criminal justice system more teeth, the Criminal Code was reformed, toughening the penalties for drug smuggling and related corruption. The Attorney General's Office also positioned rapid-response interdiction strike forces at new bases of operation throughout Mexico. Most prominent was the establishment in 1990 of the Northern Border Response Force to target cocaine air shipments from Colombia. The U.S. State Department, the Pentagon, and the DEA assisted these efforts by providing training, equipment, and intelligence.

Salinas also extended the antidrug role of the military. A new army staff section focused on drug control, and about one-third of the military's budget was devoted to the effort by the end of the 1980s. As a result of its growing antidrug mission, the military became the "supreme authority, or in some cases the only authority," in parts of some states, among them Oaxaca, Sinaloa, Jalisco, and Guerrero.[14] Militarization fit well with the new emphasis on defining drugs as a national security threat.

As the Salinas government beefed up efforts on the Mexican side of the border, U.S. drug control strategists built up interdiction efforts on their side. The shift in drug smuggling from the Southeast to the Southwest provided the main rationale for escalation. As the Bush administration reported in 1991, "The successes of interdiction forces in the southeastern United States and the Caribbean islands and Sea has caused drug smugglers to shift their focus toward Mexico as a primary transit point into the United States"; therefore, "resources have been enhanced along the Southwest border." Concretely, that meant 175 new Customs Service inspectors, 200 more Border Patrol agents, 23 more canine drug-detection teams, and increased funds for "capital assets such as fencing, ground sensors, traffic checkpoints, aerostats, and other equipment to detect smugglers."[15]

The formal designation of the region as a "High Intensity Drug Trafficking Area" in 1990 reinforced attention to the border, including additional federal antidrug assistance and enforcement initiatives. Between 1988 and 1993 the Customs Service increased the number of southwestern border inspectors by 41 percent and investigators by 21 percent. While Customs focused on the ports of entry, in 1992 the Border Patrol was designated

13. María Celia Toro, *Mexico's "War" on Drugs: Causes and Consequences* (Boulder, Colo.: Lynne Rienner, 1995), 58.

14. Roderic Ai Camp, *Generals in the Palacio: The Military in Modern Mexico* (New York: Oxford University Press, 1992), 92.

15. Office of National Drug Control Policy, *National Drug Control Strategy* (Washington, D.C., 1991), 102–3.

the lead law enforcement agency for drug interdiction between the ports of entry. New fencing projects were initiated to deter drug-laden vehicles from entering the U.S. at unauthorized crossing points.

An important institutional development was the establishment of the Southwest Border Initiative in October 1994. Its purpose was to "develop a regional strategy to investigate, prosecute and dismantle the most significant narcotics traffickers operating from Mexico."[16] To oversee its implementation, the Southwest Border Council was composed of the U.S. attorneys covering the border area and representatives from the Justice Department's Criminal Division, DEA, FBI, the Customs Service, and the INS Border Patrol.

The border also became more militarized. In November 1989, as part of the Pentagon's expanded interdiction role, Joint Task Force Six (JTF-6) was established, based at Fort Bliss, Texas. JTF-6 involved units of some seventy infantrymen armed with M-16 rifles; they were divided into camouflaged four-man teams to cover designated thirty-mile segments of the border. In FY 1990, JTF-6 conducted twenty operations in support of border drug enforcement. By FY 1992 the number of missions had increased to 408.[17]

Teams of National Guardsmen were also drafted into antidrug work in the late 1980s, deployed to remote border posts to monitor smuggling in rural areas and to ports of entry for cargo inspection. What began as a test program became a permanent presence. With the enactment of the National Defense Authorization Act for FY 1990 and 1991, Congress authorized funding for National Guard interdiction activities.[18]

APPEARANCES AND REALITIES:
THE POLITICAL SUCCESS OF A FAILING POLICY

The impressive quantitative results of the drug enforcement offensive—more arrests and seizures—were officially promoted as evidence of un-

16. Testimony of Mary Lee Warren, deputy assistant attorney general, Criminal Division, the House Subcommittee on National Security, International Affairs, and Criminal Justice Committee on Government Reform and Oversight, *Counternarcotics Efforts in Mexico and Along the Southwest Border,* 105th Cong., 1st sess., 25 February 1997, 72.

17. Oversight Hearing on Border Drug Interdiction, Senate Subcommittee on Treasury, Postal Service, and General Government, Committee on Appropriations, *Border Drug Interdiction,* 103d Cong., 1st sess., 25 February 1993, 133.

18. In the words of one guardsman engaged in border surveillance in southern California, "It's hot, it's miserable, it sucks, but this is how we make our grant money": quoted in *San Diego Union-Tribune,* 20 October 1996.

precedented U.S. and Mexican resolve and cooperation in fighting drugs.[19] During Salinas's six-year term in office, arrests nearly doubled, prominent traffickers (most notably Miguel Angel Félix Gallardo) were jailed, and principal figures in the Camarena case were convicted. Seizure levels rose sharply, prompting Mexican officials to boast that they were confiscating more drugs than any other country in the region. Indeed, in Salinas's first year in office the government seized more drugs than in the previous six years combined.[20]

Year after year the State Department's annual *International Narcotics Control Strategy Report* offered glowing reviews of Mexico's antidrug record, emphasizing the unprecedented bilateral cooperation and the results that had been achieved. Assessing the Salinas record, Robert Gelbard, the State Department's top drug control official, told the Senate Foreign Relations Committee that "Mexico's anti-drug effort has been among the most dynamic and comprehensive in the hemisphere": under Salinas, "Mexican authorities seized over 247 metric tons of cocaine, made over 100,000 drug-related arrests, and eradicated 147,000 hectares of opium poppy and marijuana crops. . . . President Salinas also established the National Counternarcotics Institute (INCD) to improve inter-agency anti-drug coordination, overcome bureaucratic obstacles and address corruption." Gelbard concluded that "these successes represent a substantial level of effort and a credible demonstration of political will."[21]

As hoped, Mexico's antidrug performance helped preserve the upbeat mood in U.S.-Mexican relations on the eve of the NAFTA vote. Salinas was apparently well aware that a positive antidrug image was a prerequisite for passage of the agreement. An internal 1992 U.S. Defense Intelligence Agency memorandum observed that "perhaps the most important of all of Salinas' motivations is his perception that a better image of Mexico will figure prominently and favorably in the outcome of ongoing free trade negotiations."[22]

U.S. officials were not passive bystanders but active collaborators in the effort to recraft Mexico's drug control image. Salinas and his American

19. Procuraduria General de la Republica, *Programa Nacional 1989–1994: Evaluacion y Seguimiento* (Mexico City, February 1993); Procuraduria General de la Republica, Instituto Nacional para el Combate a las Drogas, *Programa Nacional para el Control de Drogas, 1989– 1994: Avances y Resultados* (Mexico City, September 1994).

20. U.S. Department of State, *Department of State Dispatch,* 26 November 1990, 294.

21. Testimony of Robert Gelbard, assistant secretary of state for international narcotics and law enforcement matters, Senate Committee on Foreign Relations, *The Drug Trade in Mexico and Its Implications for U.S.-Mexican Relations,* 104th Cong., 1st sess., 8 August 1995, 67.

22. Defense Intelligence Agency, *Defense Intelligence Assessment. Mexican Counterdrug Security Forces: Problems and Prospects* (Washington, D.C., June 1992), iv (obtained through the Freedom of Information Act by the National Security Archive).

counterparts were, in a sense, on the same political stage, carrying out a carefully choreographed performance designed to project the right messages and images to an anxious domestic U.S. audience. Law enforcement agents who worked in Mexico during the Salinas years were reportedly warned by their superiors not to let the drug issue undermine progress toward a new economic relationship.[23] As a former drug policy official in the Bush administration acknowledged, "People desperately wanted drugs not to become a complicating factor for NAFTA," and another official noted that "once Bush and Salinas decided to go with NAFTA as the No. 1 goal, then everything else had to be made manageable."[24] One State Department official even conceded that his job was to make the Mexican government look good so that U.S. congressmen would be more willing to sign the trade pact.[25]

Pushing NAFTA through Congress also required deflecting concerns that opening the border to legal trade might unintentionally open it to illegal drugs. In May 1993, two members of Congress, Representatives Helen Bentley (R-Md.) and Marcy Kaptur (D-Ohio), wrote a bipartisan "Dear Colleague" letter insisting that "Congress should not approve the NAFTA deal unless it and our borders are locked tight from drug runners."[26] Their concern had been sparked by a front-page *New York Times* story reporting that Mexican traffickers were preparing to exploit the free-trade agreement as a cover for drug smuggling.[27]

At least for a time, the administration was able to push aside such worries by pointing to the apparent progress made by the joint U.S. and Mexican interdiction efforts and promising that NAFTA would further energize such efforts because it would lead to greater U.S.-Mexican antidrug cooperation. Moreover, the administration stressed that even though the border was being made more business-friendly, it was also being made more secure.[28] A $357 million upgrade of inspection stations along the border would increase the number of truck inspection docks from 130 to 902. Other initiatives involved enhanced use of detection technologies

23. *New York Times*, 11 July 1997.
24. Quoted in *New York Times*, 31 July 1995.
25. National Public Radio, *Morning Edition*, 23 May 1995.
26. *Christian Science Monitor*, 4 June 1993.
27. *Congressional Record*, 103d Cong., 1st sess., 25 May 1993, H2776.
28. "While the increase in legitimate trade across the U.S. / Mexican border could offer . . . opportunities for increased drug smuggling, the U.S. is increasing the number of U.S. Customs inspectors on the border, enhancing inspection technology, increasing coordination with other U.S. law enforcement agencies, as well as developing cooperative relationships with Mexican law enforcement agencies and with legitimate Mexican exporters": Department of State, *Administration Position Paper: NAFTA and the War on Drugs* (Washington, D.C., October 1993).

such as X-ray equipment and mobile scanners.[29] U.S. agencies were directed how to handle any worries and perceptions that NAFTA might make the border more permeable to the flow of drugs.[30] Law enforcement officials who thought NAFTA was bad for drug control were reportedly silenced.[31]

During the campaign to pass the free-trade agreement, however, drug smuggling across the border not only survived but thrived, creating a far more formidable law enforcement problem in the post-NAFTA era. As the *Economist* observed:

> During Mr. Salinas's tenure, drug bosses consolidated their fiefs. . . . American anti-drug agents knew of the spreading rot, often refusing to work with counterparts they knew to be crooked. But other American officials, keen to cement Mr. Salinas's economic reforms with the North American Free Trade Agreement, turned a blind eye, often issuing statements praising his anti-drug efforts, despite evidence to the contrary.[32]

According to one senior State Department official, U.S. Embassy staff reports from Mexico City deliberately glossed over problems of drug-related corruption in the effort to push NAFTA forward.[33]

As the Salinas government was renegotiating its economic partnership with Washington, Mexican smugglers were renegotiating the terms of their partnership with Colombia's cocaine exporters. In the beginning of that business alliance, the Mexicans had simply been paid in cash for moving Colombian cocaine across the southwestern border, $1,000–2,000 for every kilogram. But as the relationship matured and the Colombians faced intensified law enforcement pressure at home and abroad, the leverage of the Mexican smugglers grew. As a result, they increasingly demanded payment in the form of product: 40–50 percent of each cocaine shipment, which in turn expanded their own distribution networks, especially in the western parts of the United States. Thus they increased the Mexican share of cocaine profits five to ten times, dramatically changing the financial

29. Ibid.

30. For example, a 17 August 1993 Customs Service memorandum from the deputy commissioner to the commissioner (Washington, D.C., 17 August 1993) listed a number of talking points that could be used in handling public inquiries, such as highlighting that "Customs staffing was increased by 300 inspector positions in FY 92" for the southwest border, thus adding to "a gradual build-up of Customs inspectors and agent personnel since 1987."

31. Former DEA official Phil Jordan, interviewed on ABC News *Nightline,* 6 May 1997, claimed that DEA agents were ordered to keep quiet about NAFTA's potential negative consequences.

32. *Economist,* 16 December 1995, 38–39.

33. Author interview with State Department official, Washington, D.C., 2 August 1996.

stakes of smuggling across the southwestern border.[34] At the same time, Mexican smugglers were rapidly taking over the booming U.S. market for methamphetamines—thanks in part to U.S. law enforcement crackdowns on domestic producers.

Mexico's growing stake in the cocaine trade produced more sophisticated and organized smuggling organizations along the border's transportation hubs, the most prominent of which were the so-called Gulf, Tijuana, and Juárez cartels. Their meteoric rise would later lead the head of the DEA to describe them as "the premier law enforcement threat facing the United States."[35] According to Eduardo Valle, who resigned in protest as personal adviser to the Mexican attorney general in May 1994, Mexico's leading drug traffickers had become "driving forces, pillars even, of our economic growth."[36] The Mexican government calculated that the gross revenues of Mexican drug-smuggling organizations reached $30 billion in 1994;[37] U.S. officials estimated the profits at $10 billion.[38] (For comparison, it should be noted that Mexico's most important legal export, oil, generated $7.4 billion in 1993.)[39] Such figures, of course, necessarily represent "guesstimates," but even the most conservative numbers indicate that the drug trade had become a major economic force in Mexico.

Ironically, the operational achievements of the U.S. and Mexican antidrug campaigns during the Salinas years were actually aided by an expanding drug trade: well-publicized increases in seizures and arrests on both sides of the border were partly made possible by the fact that there were more drugs to seize and smugglers to arrest. Similarly, record eradication levels were facilitated by bumper crops of marijuana and opium poppy. In other words, the boom in the drug trade also meant a boom for law enforcement. As Barry McCaffrey, the White House drug policy director told a congressional committee in 1996, "The positive news is that our agents and inspectors are seizing huge amounts of drugs. . . . Seizures on the southwest border climbed dramatically from 1991 to 1995": by 50 percent for cocaine, 100 percent for heroin, and 150 percent for marijuana.[40] He emphasized that drug seizures by the Mexican government were up as

34. *New York Times,* 11 July 1997.

35. Quoted in *Washington Post,* 30 March 1997.

36. Quoted in *Mexican Insights* (Washington, D.C.: Washington Office on Latin America, July 1995), 45.

37. *Excelsior* (Mexico City), 26 August 1995.

38. General Accounting Office, *Drug Control: Counternarcotics Efforts in Mexico (Appendix II: Comments from the Drug Enforcement Administration)* (Washington, D.C., June 1996), 26.

39. *La Jornada* (Mexico City), 16 May 1994.

40. Testimony of Barry R. McCaffrey, director of the Office of National Drug Control Policy, Senate Judiciary Committee, *Drug Interdiction on the U.S.-Mexico Border,* 104th Cong., 2d sess., 31 July 1996.

well. Left conveniently unmentioned was whether these results were having any real deterrent effect on smuggling across the border or any impact on the price and availability of drugs on U.S. streets.

Impressive drug enforcement statistics masked the fact that the Mexican crackdown was selective: old guard smugglers were targeted (especially those connected to Colombia's Medellín cartel), while the business of other smugglers (especially those connected to Colombia's rising Cali cartel) expanded. Thus, record arrest and seizure statistics during the Salinas years did not lead to less smuggling but simply created openings for more aggressive smugglers on the rise. For example, the Arellano Félix brothers, leaders of the Tijuana cartel, moved up as the government jailed traffickers such as Rafaél Caro Quintero, Félix Gallardo, and Chapo Guzmán.[41]

Nevertheless, what mattered politically was that Mexico and the United States formally embraced the same policy goals: on the one hand, market liberalization; on the other, a renewed and expanded commitment to drug criminalization. Salinas, a Harvard-educated technocrat, was viewed in the United States as an ideal partner in pushing these goals forward and forging a new bilateral relationship. As one official in the U.S. Embassy in Mexico City put it, "We liked Salinas because he wasn't anti-American." He was "someone we could work with."[42]

Yet the feedback effects of the policy initiatives during the Salinas years made managing the drug trade and bilateral relations over the drug issue increasingly difficult in the post-NAFTA era—provoking further calls for enforcement escalation.

FROM INCREASED LAW ENFORCEMENT TO INCREASED CORRUPTION

Although the Salinas antidrug offensive helped pacify U.S. critics and paved the way for the passage of NAFTA, it had the particularly perverse result on the ground of encouraging more drug-related corruption. As more government resources were devoted to drug control, smugglers responded by devoting more resources to paying off those doing the controlling. Thus, drug-related corruption reflected not only the weakness of the Mexican state but also its power: law enforcement had to be bribed because it could not be entirely bypassed or bullied. In order to stay in business, drug smugglers had to pay a higher price for an essential state service: the non-enforcement of the law.

The problem in Mexico was exacerbated by the fact that when Salinas

41. Sebastian Rotella, *Twilight on the Line: Underworlds and Politics at the U.S.-Mexico Border* (New York: Norton, 1998), 136.
42. Author interview, Narcotics Affairs Section, U.S. Embassy, Mexico City, 16 July 1997.

took office, he did not reform the Mexican criminal justice system but simply expanded the size and power of an already corruption-plagued policing apparatus. His top appointments, according to Peter Lupsha, produced a "law enforcement power bloc with deep connections to prior corrupt administrations, agencies and organizations."[43] For example, Salinas appointed as attorney general Enrique Alvarez del Castillo, who had been the governor of the state of Jalisco and under whose governorship the drug trade had thrived and traffickers operated with little to fear from authorities.[44]

The extent of drug-related corruption is revealed by the series of high-profile murders and scandals (including the arrest of Raúl Salinas, the president's brother) which have deeply shaken the Mexican political system in recent years. My primary purpose here is not to focus on the mystery, intrigue, and speculation that necessarily surround these controversial events but rather to show how they have helped propel an increasingly militarized escalation of drug control.

At its core, drug corruption is a cost of doing business. In the case of Mexico, a study by the Autonomous National University in Mexico City calculated that cocaine traffickers spent as much as $460 million on bribery in 1993—far more than the annual budget of the Mexican Attorney General's Office—whereas in 1983, they had spent between $1.5 and $3.2 million on bribery. (These calculations were derived from a widely used model that assumes a certain degree of corruption in trafficking nations: $1,000 in payoffs for each kilogram of cocaine.)[45]

A useful way to make sense of drug corruption is to view bribes and payoffs as the equivalent of paying a tax. Levels of corruption—the tax rate—often depend on the intensity of the drug enforcement effort: as enforcement increases, so too does the smuggler's need to corrupt those who are doing the enforcing (the tax collectors). Thus, increased drug enforcement capacity, while failing to deter the drug trade significantly, successfully increases the capacity to tax the trade in the form of corruption. Smugglers who pay the tax are less pressured by the tax collectors than those who do not. One senior Mexican official during the Salinas administration explained that drug enforcement agents "receive money from one group of traffickers and they cannot act against people from

43. Peter Lupsha, "Drug Lords and Narco-Corruption: The Players Change but the Game Continues," in *War on Drugs: Studies in the Failure of U.S. Narcotics Policy*, ed. Alfred W. McCoy and Alan A. Block (Boulder, Colo.: Westview, 1992), 191.

44. *Los Angeles Times*, 7 January 1989.

45. Samuel González Ruiz, Ernesto Lopez Portillo, and José Arturo Yanez, *Seguridad Publica en Mexico: Problemas, Perspectivas, y Propuestas* (Mexico City: UNAM, 1994), 73.

that group. But they have their hands free to arrest people from other groups."[46]

This selective enforcement is pragmatic: officials can perform their job—seizing drugs and arresting smugglers—while also collecting taxes from the drug trade. Those smugglers with the most resources and connections are the ones most able to afford the corruption tax, whereas the smaller smuggling entrepreneurs are treated as tax evaders. Not surprisingly, then, it is the small-time smugglers that have most often been "audited" and penalized. Thus, while having little impact on the overall drug flow, enforcement has helped to weed out amateur smugglers and to inflate arrest statistics.

The financial rewards of drug enforcement have created enormous competition within law enforcement agencies for assignment to key posts along the smuggling corridors. Eduardo Valle, who left the attorney general's office toward the end of the Salinas administration, claims that while he was in office the top Mexican drug enforcement posts were auctioned off to the highest bidder. The price of a particular law enforcement position, he says, depends on changes in drug smuggling routes along the border: "In Coahuila, for example, there are four or five entrances into the United States. If one crossing point is closed, the price of the federal police chief's position in that area goes down because the post is irrelevant, but the price of the police chief positions in other places goes up. This is openly discussed inside the federal police."[47]

The case of Mario Ruiz Massieu, Salinas's top antidrug prosecutor between March and November 1994, provides a glimpse into how the system of drug corruption can be organized. Federal prosecutors and police commanders allegedly paid Ruiz Massieu as much as $1 million to be assigned to profitable posts along the border and in other major drug areas. Officials brought him suitcases containing up to $150,000 in regular kickbacks. One official familiar with Ruiz Massieu's operation described it as a "franchising system."[48] Nor, apparently, did the selling of posts cease after his departure. In 1995 it was reported in the Mexican press that border area posts were being sold for up to $500,000.[49]

The higher the law enforcement position, the higher the payoff. For example, a notebook recovered from the smuggling organization run by Juan García Abrego of the Gulf cartel included a list of payoffs: $1 million to the national commander of Mexico's Federal Judicial Police; $500,000

---

46. Quoted in *New York Times*, 20 June 1993.
47. National Public Radio, *Morning Edition*, 23 May 1995.
48. Quoted in *Los Angeles Times*, 16 June 1995.
49. *Excelsior* (Mexico City), 7 September 1995.

to the force's operations chief; $100,000 to the federal police commander in the city of Matamoros. García Abrego's cousin Francisco Pérez testified in a 1994 federal trial in Texas that between 1988 and 1991 he had delivered $500,000 to Javier Coello Trejo, Mexico's deputy attorney general. Coello was eventually dismissed but never charged.[50]

Beyond providing corrupt state officials with a share of the profits, as Peter Lupsha explains, the trafficker is

> Expected to assist the police and the political system by providing grist for the judicial mill, as well as public relations materials to give U.S. drug enforcers. Thus, while the trafficker could gain protection and warning information, the police could gain credit, praise, and promotions; the political system gained campaign monies and control; and the U.S., statistics, to justify a job well done.[51]

This symbiotic relationship has been volatile, given changes in government leadership, the transfer or promotion of key officials, and violent competition between smuggling organizations over transportation routes.[52] This volatility was evident, for example, in the rise and demise of one of Mexico's leading traffickers, García Abrego, who was a major beneficiary of the arrest of Angel Félix Gallardo early in the Salinas administration. But García Abrego's trafficking operation, which flourished during the Salinas era, lost high-level protection after President Ernesto Zedillo Ponce de León entered office in late 1994 and soon lost market share to its Tijuana and Juárez competitors. Having fallen out of favor, he became a hunted fugitive. By the time he was arrested in early 1996 and extradited to the United States, his business was in shambles.[53] His capture was nevertheless applauded by the United States and Mexico as a sign of official resolve in the antidrug campaign. This high-profile arrest, meanwhile, created new opportunities for other smuggling organizations, especially the Juárez cartel, headed by Amado Carrillo Fuentes.

Corruption scandals have resulted in the firing or transferring of individual officers and, at times, the disbanding of entire agencies and the creation of new ones. A report from the Mexican Attorney General's Office indicates that some 400 agents of the Federal Judicial Police (over 10 percent of total personnel) were fired or suspended on drug-related charges between mid-1992 and mid-1995.[54] On 14 August 1996, 737 federal law

50. *New York Times*, 12 May 1996.
51. Lupsha, "Drug Lords and Narco-Corruption," 182.
52. Ibid.
53. *New York Times*, 12 May 1996.
54. Cited in Andres Oppenheimer, *Bordering on Chaos: Guerillas, Stockbrokers, Politicians, and Mexico's Road to Prosperity* (Boston: Little, Brown, 1996), 302.

enforcement officers were dismissed (including Horacio Brunt, the celebrated police commander who had captured the head of the Gulf cartel), and an additional 270 employees of the Attorney General's Office were fired between December 1996 and August 1997.[55] Such mass firings, however, have been overshadowed by the magnitude of the problem: the Mexican attorney general estimated in 1996 that "70 to 80 percent" of the judicial police force was corrupt.[56] Moreover, many fired police officers were rehired in other regions of the country.[57] Others simply joined the criminal underworld full time. The Mexican Ministry of the Interior estimated in an internal report that by 1995 there were about 900 armed criminal bands, more than half of whose members were current or former law enforcement agents.[58]

FROM INCREASED CORRUPTION TO MILITARIZED ESCALATION

The response of the Zedillo government to the growing corruption problem was to turn to the military.[59] Its antidrug role, though enhanced during the Salinas years, expanded much further under Zedillo. "In the past, there was always a reluctance to allow the military to play a stronger role," noted one U.S. official in 1995. "But with the Zedillo administration, that mind-set has dissolved."[60] This new reliance on the military reaffirmed the Mexican government's definition of drug trafficking as "the most serious danger to national security."[61] And it was greeted with enthusiasm by U.S. officials in Washington and at the embassy in Mexico City.[62]

In order to give the military new law enforcement powers, Zedillo modified the constitution and criminal codes. Generals were put in charge of the Federal Judicial Police, the National Institute to Combat Drugs, and the Center for the Planning of Drug Control. An active-duty officer also headed the uniformed branch of the Mexican federal Customs Service.

55. Office of National Drug Control Policy, *Report to Congress*, vol. 1, *United States and Mexico Counterdrug Cooperation* (Washington, D.C., September 1997), 35.

56. Quoted in *Boston Globe*, 1 September 1996.

57. Associated Press, 29 September 1996.

58. Cited in Oppenheimer, *Bordering on Chaos*, 301.

59. On the Mexican military in the 1990s, see Raul Benitez Manaut, "Mexico: La Nueva Dimension de las Fuerzas Armadas en los Años Noventa," *Fuerzas Armadas y Sociedad* 11, no. 3 (1996): 8–17.

60. Quoted in *International Herald Tribune*, 25 May 1995.

61. Mexican Government, *National Drug Control Program: 1995–2000* (Mexico City, October 1995), 6.

62. Author interview, Narcotics Affairs Section, U.S. Embassy, Mexico City, 16 July 1997.

Moreover, the military increasingly ran the Center for National Security and Investigation (the federal intelligence agency).

By early 1998, military personnel occupied top law enforcement posts in two-thirds of Mexico's states.[63] For example, more than one hundred military personnel were brought into the federal Attorney General's Office in the northern state of Chihuahua and others were engaged for similar functions in the border state of Tamaulipas. In some states, such as Nuevo Leon, the Federal Judicial Police forces were entirely replaced by soldiers.[64] Overall, by 1998 some 40 percent of the 180,000-member army was reportedly focused on drug control.[65] Along the U.S.-Mexico border, where the militarization of Mexican law enforcement is most pronounced, there have been "numerous incidents" in which the Mexican army's close proximity to the U.S. Border Patrol has involved "several unauthorized entries of armed Mexican patrols into U.S. territory."[66] The Mexican secretaries of defense and navy now acknowledge that drug control has become the primary mission of their services.[67]

The militarization of drug control in Mexico has also meant a greater militarization of U.S.-Mexico relations and new cross-border military ties. Interaction between the U.S. and Mexican armed forces, extremely limited in the past, has become more intimate through military assistance and training for antidrug programs.[68] A bilateral working group for military issues, created following the visit of Secretary of Defense William Perry in October 1995 (the first trip to Mexico by a U.S. secretary of defense), included among its functions cooperation on drug issues. And the following April his Mexican counterpart, General Enrique Cervantes Aguirre, visited the United States. In FY 1997 more than 1,500 Mexican military personnel were scheduled for training in an expanded Department of Defense counternarcotics program. In addition, the CIA has provided instruction, resources, and operational support for a Mexican army intelligence unit: the Center for Anti-Narcotics Investigations—CIAN.[69] These developments are particularly remarkable, given that until the 1980s Mexican military manuals depicted the United States as Mexico's enemy.[70]

63. *Economist*, 8 March 1998, pp. 44–46.

64. Donald E. Schulz, *Between a Rock and a Hard Place: The United States, Mexico, and the Agony of National Security*, Strategic Studies Institute Special Report (Carlisle Barracks, Pa.: Strategic Studies Institute, U.S. Army War College, 24 June 1997), 4.

65. See George W. Grayson, "Civilians Order Army Out of the Barracks," *Hemisfile* 9, no. 3 (1998): 8.

66. Department of State, *International Narcotics Control Strategy Report* (Washington, D.C., March 1997).

67. Department of State, *International Narcotics Control Strategy Report* (Washington D.C., March 1999).

68. Author interview, Narcotics Affairs Section, U.S. Embassy, Mexico City, 16 July 1997.

69. Grayson, "Civilians Order Army Out of the Barracks," 8.

70. Schulz, *Between a Rock and a Hard Place*, 17.

But even as militarization has projected an image of Mexico's heightened commitment to drug deterrence, the expanded military role in drug control (and thus proximity to drug smugglers) has also increased the risk of greater corruption within the military, which—past experience suggests—is not necessarily less corruptible than the police. In one of the most notorious cases of military corruption, as ten agents from Mexico's Federal Judicial Police attempted to apprehend smugglers delivering 800 pounds of cocaine from a small airplane on a remote airstrip in the state of Veracruz in late 1991, members of the Mexican army opened fire on the agents, killing seven of them. The traffickers escaped. The U.S. ambassador to Mexico described the incident as "a regrettable accident."[71] A videotape made by a U.S. Customs surveillance flight overhead, however, indicated that the Mexican soldiers were protecting the traffickers.[72]

A series of drug-related scandals in recent years have further exposed the growing corruption problem within the military. In February 1997 the head of the federal antidrug agency, General Jesús Gutiérrez Rebollo, was arrested on charges of working for the Juárez cartel. The agency, which had been patterned after the DEA and was the source of much U.S. praise when it opened in 1993, was quickly dismantled. It has now been rebuilt as the Special Prosecutor's Office for Crimes against Health (FEADS).

Just a few weeks before the scandal, the White House drug policy director, Barry McCaffrey, had described the general as "an honest man who is a no-nonsense field commander of the Mexican army who's now been sent to bring to the police force the same kind of aggressiveness and reputation he had in uniform."[73] Indeed, no other army commander had displayed more antidrug initiative. The problem was its selective focus, largely leaving the Juárez cartel untouched while targeting other trafficking groups. "He was showing results," one U.S. official had noted.[74] Apparently, these results inhibited further scrutiny at the time.

The news of the general's arrest caught American officials off guard. According to one U.S. embassy official in Mexico City, concerns over military corruption had rarely been mentioned in staff meetings prior to the affair.[75] Following the arrest, officials in Mexico City and Washington rushed into damage-control mode. Mexican Attorney General Jorge Madrazo Cuellar promised a massive overhaul of the criminal justice system to fight drug trafficking and organized crime. President Zedillo said that the corruption case revealed the seriousness of narcotics crime and

71. *New York Times,* 11 July 1997.

72. Kevin Jack Riley, *Snowjob? The War against International Cocaine Trafficking* (New Brunswick, N.J.: Transaction, 1996), 231.

73. Press conference with Barry McCaffrey, director, Office of National Drug Control Policy, and Jorge Madrazo, Mexican attorney general, Washington, D.C., 29 January 1997.

74. Quoted in *New York Times,* 11 July 1997.

75. Author interview, Narcotics Affairs Section, U.S. Embassy, Mexico City, 16 July 1997.

that the government would "have to take measures never seen before in our country to stop it."[76] Meanwhile, President Bill Clinton tried to give the general's arrest the most positive spin possible: "They're obviously saying to the world and the people of Mexico, we will not tolerate the corruption . . . even if it's at the highest level."[77] Robert Gelbard, the State Department's top antidrug official, offered a similar interpretation: "If the Gutiérrez Rebollo arrest revealed just how deeply rooted corruption is in Mexican counter-drug institutions, it also showed unprecedented political courage by President Zedillo. . . . This is precisely the kind of progress we are trying to encourage."[78]

Yet this scandal, although an unusually high-profile one, proved not to be an isolated incident. The next month, General Alfredo Navarro Lara was arrested for offering $1 million a month to the top federal justice official in Baja California on behalf of the Tijuana drug cartel.[79] And a 1997 White House report indicated that thirty-four senior Mexican military officers had been targeted for disciplinary action as a result of drug-related corruption.[80]

The Mexican government's response to such corruption, however, has been to reinforce the militarization trend. As the head of the organized crime unit within the Mexican Attorney General's Office has explained it, putting the military on the front lines of drug control is a big risk, but there is no alternative, given the deepening corruption within the police forces during the past decade.[81] Other officials have acknowledged that there are human rights risks but argue that the military can be no worse than the police already are.[82] Their views echo a common perception in Mexico that the military is a lesser evil than the police.

The militarization of Mexican drug control has also been oriented toward impressing an external audience.[83] It has sold well in Washington

76. *New York Times*, 25 February 1997.

77. Quoted in *San Diego Union-Tribune*, 21 February 1997.

78. Testimony of Robert Gelbard, assistant secretary of state for international narcotics and law enforcement matters, Senate Subcommittee on Western Hemisphere and Peace Corps Affairs, Foreign Relations Committee, *Mexican and American Responses to the International Narcotics Threat*, 105th Cong., 1st sess., 12 March 1997.

79. Andrew Reding, "Facing Political Reality in Mexico," *Washington Quarterly* 20, no. 4 (1997): 103–17.

80. Office of National Drug Control Policy, *Report to Congress*, 1:35.

81. Author interview with Samuel González Ruiz, director, Organized Crime Unit of the Mexican Attorney General's Office, Mexico City, 16 July 1997.

82. Author interview with Miguél Ruiz-Cabañas, Ministry of Foreign Affairs, Mexico City, 18 July 1997.

83. According to one Mexican official, militarization is primarily driven by the need to appease the United States. Author interview with Mexican Embassy official, Washington, D.C., 3 June 1997.

because it sends a strong signal that the Mexican government considers drug trafficking a serious national security threat. Such signaling has often come at politically opportune moments. For example, early in the morning of 1 March 1996—the day of the deadline for the Clinton administration's decision on whether or not to certify Mexico as fully complying with U.S. drug control objectives—Mexican troops were deployed in a highly visible sweep of Tijuana neighborhoods in search of the Arellano Félix brothers, leaders of the Tijuana drug cartel. By the end of the day, Mexico had received the certification blessing from Washington, and the troops returned to barracks. The next year the ante was upped: one week before the U.S. certification deadline, Mexico replaced the entire federal police force in the border state of Baja with military personnel. "Obviously, the Mexican government wants to satisfy parts of the U.S. government by doing something spectacular before the certification," observed Victor Clark Alfaro, a prominent human rights leader in Tijuana.[84]

FROM DRUG CERTIFICATION RITUALS TO FURTHER ESCALATION

It was in 1986 that the U.S. Congress pushed through a law requiring that the State Department provide an annual report card for drug-producing and -exporting countries, indicating the extent of their cooperation with U.S. antidrug objectives. Countries labeled as noncooperative would be "decertified," resulting in material and nonmaterial penalties: aid cutoffs, votes against loans from multilateral lending agencies, loss of trade preferences, and the stigma of being branded a "narco-state." Alternatively, the president could decertify a country but opt for a national-interest waiver—meaning that the material penalties would not be imposed but the stigma of the decertification label would remain.

In reality, only a few countries have been fully decertified, and these tend to be countries Washington has few ties to, such as Iran and Syria. Nevertheless, the certification process has powerfully conditioned the practice and politics of drug control. Even if rarely fully enforced, the law has framed the drug debate and kept the issue on the policy agenda. By establishing an annual review process that commands significant political attention and media coverage, the law guarantees that the antidrug performance of countries such as Mexico will be on Washington's radar screen. The certification process also shifts attention away from the domestic demand for drugs and toward the foreign supply.

Further, the focus on supply reduction has reinforced political and bureaucratic incentives to rely on misleading measures of cooperation.

84. Quoted in Associated Press, 21 February 1997.

As one U.S. antidrug official put it, beefing up the tools of the supply-reduction effort—as in Mexico's acceptance of more helicopters from the United States—becomes an "end goal," regardless of what is actually accomplished.[85]

Moreover, because the certification process rewards the most immediate and visible operational "successes"—arrests and seizures—drug-exporting countries tend to prioritize the law enforcement efforts that generate these results. Policy initiatives that have longer-term but less visible effects, such as judicial reform, may be neglected. Regardless of what the drug war statistics actually indicate, a positive image of effort is what gets a passing grade in the certification game. As one U.S. official has candidly remarked, "If I were a Mexican official, I would do the same thing: give the Americans the statistics that will make them happy."[86]

The certification process has produced heated criticism, not only from foreign governments (who consider it patronizing and hypocritical) but also at home. Calling it a charade, Senator Christopher Dodd (D-Conn.) has pointed out that "if we were to subject our own nation to this very test we apply to other countries, we wouldn't pass it." The certification process, he said, "places us in a very silly situation year in and year out where we pick winners and losers where no one is a winner." Since no country is actually "fully cooperating" with the United States, the certification law "creates the kind of sham situations we find ourselves in." The senator has urged a reconsideration of the law: "It's great for press releases, it's great for speeches and so forth, but I don't think it's helping us substantially in advancing the common international efforts that have to be waged if we're going to be successful in our war against the proliferation of narcotics."[87]

Nevertheless, policymakers have so far been reluctant to change the law for fear of the reputational costs. As Representative Lee Hamilton (D-Ind.) has put it, "We cannot be seen as politicians who are weak on drugs."[88] Thus, certification has had a lock-in effect: once established, it has proved extraordinarily difficult to discard or even modify.

During the Salinas era, Mexico successfully jumped through the certification hoops with little serious political opposition. Increases in drugs seized, crops eradicated, and smugglers arrested proved sufficient to keep congressional critics in Washington at bay. Other countries, such as Peru, Bolivia, and Colombia, received noticeably more scrutiny. In the post-

85. Author interview, Narcotics Affairs Section, U.S. Embassy, Mexico City, 17 July 1997.
86. Ibid.
87. Statements of Christopher Dodd, Senate Committee on Banking, Housing, and Urban Affairs, *The Narcotics Threat to the United States through Mexico*, 104th Cong., 2d sess., 28 March 1996.
88. Comments of Lee Hamilton, press conference on the certification process, National Press Club, Washington, D.C., 6 February 1998.

Salinas era, however, revelations of deepening corruption and the expanding power of Mexico's drug-smuggling organizations pushed Mexico to center stage in the Washington certification debate, putting the administration in an increasingly uncomfortable position: to decertify Mexico would contradict the entire thrust of Clinton's Mexico policy and deeply strain cross-border relations; to do nothing would invite congressional allegations that the president was not taking the drug problem seriously. As a way out of this straitjacket, in 1996 the administration opted to display its antidrug resolve and distract attention from Mexico by decertifying a more distant country that it could more easily afford to alienate: Colombia. Although the press and critics viewed this move as hypocritical and cynical, within the White House it was considered a political success; Clinton, it seemed, had dodged a bullet.[89]

But the decision to praise Mexico and punish Colombia, though it may have worked politically, further eroded the credibility of the administration's drug performance reviews. At a heated congressional hearing over the decision to certify Mexico that year, Senator Carol Moseley-Braun (D-Ill.) commented that the certification process "has nothing, zippo, to do with the truth with regard to narcotics enforcement. To suggest that it docs is why you have these Senators bouncing off the walls here." Senator Robert Bennett (R-Utah) explained it in broader but equally blunt political terms:

> The certification is clearly a joke, if the purpose is to determine what is going on in Mexico. At the same time, I understand why it was done. It was done because the President felt that we could not undercut President Zedillo to the point where the problem would get worse, so we lied. . . . We can't de-certify Mexico. We have to lie about what is going on because our relationship with Mexico is so important that we can't let it go down the tubes.

Other senators, however, less concerned about preserving the overall bilateral relationship, continued to protest the administration's certification decision. As Pete Domenici (R-N.Mex.) exclaimed, "We can't continue to let our borders be invaded the way they are."[90]

Scrambling to contain and respond to the political fallout from the 1996 certification debate, in March the Clinton and Zedillo administrations created the High-Level Contact Group against Drugs, composed of a team of senior U.S. and Mexican officials. Among its main objectives was the design of a bilateral cooperative antidrug strategy to improve cross-border

---

89. Author interview with former Clinton foreign policy adviser, 13 December 1996.

90. Senate, Committee on Banking, Housing, and Urban Affairs, *The Narcotics Threat to the United States through Mexico: Hearing*, 104th Cong., 2d sess., 28 March 1996.

institutional coordination and to assess joint initiatives and their results.[91] In other words, as an increasingly restless U.S. Congress demanded more results, Clinton and Zedillo officials mobilized to collaborate in delivering a more persuasive performance. To call the performance collaborative, however, is not to suggest that it was not coercive: pressure from Congress provided the administration with the leverage to gain law enforcement concessions from Mexico. One Mexican official described it as a "good cop, bad cop" routine: Congress played bad cop, blasting Mexico on its antidrug record, and then Clinton officials played good cop, negotiating with Mexico to show progress on the antidrug front to pacify Congress.[92]

Mexico's antidrug performance, which included the implementation of new and expanded anti-organized crime legislation, received a positive grade in the administration's March 1997 certification review.[93] But the ensuing congressional reaction was even more hostile than that of the previous year—partly because the certification decision came on the heels of the news that Mexico's top antidrug official, General Gutiérrez Rebollo, was on the payroll of the very smugglers he was in charge of fighting. The embarrassing corruption scandal, which could not have come at a worse time for Mexico, provided important political ammunition for an emerging bipartisan coalition of Mexico critics on Capitol Hill.

To appease Congress and avoid a deeper diplomatic rift with Mexico, senior administration officials negotiated with Senate leaders on a resolution that required the White House to issue a progress report by the following September outlining new U.S.-Mexico achievements on the antidrug front. This resolution included demands that progress be made in dismantling drug-smuggling organizations, strengthening ties between U.S. and Mexican law enforcement agencies, increasing joint patrols on the border, and tackling corruption.[94] In short, the price paid to get Mexico through the certification hoops was to promise a bigger and better antidrug performance.

Thus, the dynamics of the certification process have pushed for further escalation. Even if the quantitative results—arrests and seizures made, crops eradicated, new laws passed, and bilateral agreements signed—have had little impact in significantly reducing smuggling, they have been politically sold as expressions of antidrug resolve. "This is not about what Mexico has done," one administration official candidly noted. "This is about convincing the Hill that whatever Mexico has done is enough."[95] Es-

91. Office of National Drug Control Policy, Executive Office of the President, *U.S./Mexico Bi-National Drug Threat Assessment* (Washington, D.C., and Mexico City, May 1997).

92. Author interview with Mexican Embassy official, Washington, D.C., 3 June 1997.

93. "Ley Federal Contra la Delincuencia Organizada," *Diario Oficial,* 7 November 1996.

94. *Los Angeles Times,* 21 March 1997.

95. Quoted in *New York Times,* 14 February 1999.

calation, in other words, has had less to do with actual deterrence than with generating the kind of statistical indicators necessary to make it through the annual certification ritual.

Armed with such statistics, the administration reported to Congress in September 1997 that eradication and seizures, "while not absolute measures of political will or operational effectiveness, are nonetheless valid indicators of a government's commitment to fighting drugs. In each year since 1994, Mexico has increased the quantity of illegal drugs seized and led the world in destruction of illegal drug crops."[96] And testifying before a Senate committee that fall, Barry McCaffrey reviewed a long list of accomplishments resulting from increased U.S.-Mexico cooperation and concluded:

> In the last two years, the level of cooperation on drugs has been phenomenal to the point that it would clearly . . . rank as one of the most dramatic transformations I've seen in the region in the last 30 years. . . . we started with almost no contact, military-to-military, police-to-police, no extradition, no money-laundering agreements, no legislation in Mexico that could deal with the problem. Now there's considerable.[97]

When statistics fail to impress adequately, administration officials point to "cooperation" itself as the most important accomplishment. As the State Department's James P. Rubin explained in evaluating Mexico's antidrug performance in February 1999, it is a country's cooperation in the drug war that counts, and "there's a difference between cooperation and success."[98] Regardless of the low results, he said, Mexican officials are "cooperating more closely with the United States at virtually every level than ever before."[99]

The Mexican government has since become more assertive in displaying its antidrug resolve prior to the certification decision, even spending $100,000 a month to hire three major Washington lobbying firms.[100] In February 1999, Zedillo dispatched his interior minister to Washington to highlight a new $550 million high-tech initiative to secure the country's borders against drug smuggling.[101] Much of that spending, he announced,

---

96. Office of National Drug Control Policy, *Report to Congress,* 1:3.

97. Testimony of Barry R. McCaffrey, director of the Office on National Drug Control Policy, joint hearing of Senate Foreign Relations Committee and Senate Caucus on International Narcotics Control, *U.S. and Mexican Counterdrug Efforts since Certification,* 105th Cong., 1st sess., 29 October 1997.

98. Quoted in *Economist,* 20 February 1999.

99. Quoted in *New York Times,* 14 February 1999.

100. *New York Times,* 2 February 1999.

101. *Financial Times,* 15 February 1999.

would go toward purchasing infrared cameras, special X-ray machines, and satellite communications gear, as well as more helicopters and planes for the country's antidrug air fleet.[102] At a congressional hearing following the decision to certify Mexico, a senior State Department official pointed out that these antidrug expenditures were especially impressive because they came at a time when Mexico's federal budget was the most austere in decades.[103]

HARDENING THE BORDER IN THE AGE OF FREE TRADE

Although NAFTA has helped turn the border into a bigger bridge for legal trade, some of its feedback effects have helped reinforce political calls to barricade the border against the illegal drug trade. The predicament facing U.S. law enforcement strategists is that NAFTA has made the task of border interdiction more difficult and at the same time has drawn heightened political and media attention to the deficiencies of the interdiction effort.

Ironically, the problem has been partly self-created. Past law enforcement initiatives not only pushed cocaine smuggling from the Southeast to the Southwest but also pushed it from the air to the ground. Smugglers have adapted by increasingly hiding their drug shipments within the rising volume of commercial trucks, railcars, and passenger vehicles crossing the border. Hence, the NAFTA-encouraged boom in cross-border traffic has had the side effect of creating a much more challenging job for those border officials expected to weed out the illegitimate flows from the legitimate ones—a challenge that has in turn provided the rationale for a further infusion of law enforcement resources at the ports of entry. As the 1999 *National Drug Control Strategy Report* explained, "Rapidly growing commerce between the United States and Mexico will complicate our efforts to keep drugs out of cross-border traffic. Since the southwest border is presently the most porous of the nation's borders, it is there that we must mount a determined coordinated effort to stop the flow of drugs."[104]

Concern that smugglers might benefit from NAFTA was deliberately not discussed during the negotiations over the free-trade accord in the early 1990s. "This was in the 'too hot to handle' category," noted Gary Huff-

102. *Washington Post,* 5 February 1999.

103. Testimony of Rand Beers, assistant secretary of state for international narcotics and law enforcement affairs, House Subcommittee on Criminal Justice, Drug Policy and Human Resources, Government Reform Committee, *Oversight of U.S.-Mexico Counternarcotics Efforts,* 106th Cong., 1st sess., 4 March 1999.

104. Office of National Drug Control Policy, *National Drug Control Strategy Report* (Washington, D.C., 1999), 69–70.

bauer of the Institute for International Economics, but "it's a painfully obvious problem."[105] An internal report written by an intelligence officer at the U.S. Embassy in Mexico City claimed that cocaine traffickers were establishing factories, warehouses, and trucking companies as fronts in anticipation of the expected boom in cross-border commerce: they "intend to maximize their legitimate business enterprises within the auspices of the new U.S.-Mexico free trade agreement."[106] Some traffickers reportedly even hired trade consultants to determine what products move most swiftly through border inspection under NAFTA guidelines. "They have very specific issues," noted Craig Chretien when he was the special agent in charge of the DEA's San Diego office. "Does a perishable get through quicker than a load of steel? What kind of cargoes get through faster than others?"[107]

Mexico has deregulated its trucking industry, meaning licensed trucks can travel anywhere within the country without inspections, and under NAFTA guidelines Mexican truckers will eventually be able to travel throughout the United States and Canada as well. On the U.S. side of the border the road network in the Southwest is being improved to handle more than a doubling of current traffic levels. Yet as early as October 1992 an internal DEA report predicted that the lifting of trucking restrictions would "prove to be a definite boon to both the legitimate food industry, and to drug smugglers who conceal their illegal shipments in trucks transporting fruits and vegetables from Mexico to U.S. markets" and that "the projected overhaul of the Mexican road system [would] expedite the exportation of both legitimate and illegitimate crops."[108]

The sheer volume of border crossings has provided an ideal environment for drug smuggling. In 1995 the DEA estimated that most cocaine traveled through regular ports of entry in commercial trucks and passenger vehicles.[109] One truck pulled over near San Diego, for example, was smuggling eight tons of cocaine stuffed into cans of jalapeño peppers.[110]

On any given day, 220,000 vehicles flow across the border into the U.S. from Mexico. Only nine large tractor-trailers loaded with cocaine would satisfy the nation's drug demand for one year.[111] U.S. border officials

---

105. Quoted in *New York Times*, 24 May 1993.

106. Ibid.

107. Quoted in *New York Times*, 30 July 1995.

108. Drug Enforcement Administration, *The New Agricultural Reform Program and Illicit Cultivations in Mexico* (Washington, D.C., 14 October 1992) (obtained by the National Security Archive through the Freedom of Information Act).

109. *Los Angeles Times*, 12 February 1995.

110. *New York Times*, 24 May 1993.

111. Testimony of Alan D. Bersin, U.S. attorney for the Southern District of California, House Subcommittee on Immigration and Claims, Committee on the Judiciary, *Border Security and Deterring Illegal Entry into the United States*, 105th Cong., 1st sess., 23 April 1997, 17.

searched more than a million commercial trucks and railway cars crossing from Mexico in 1997 and found cocaine in only six.[112] Clearly, the enforcement challenge is the equivalent of finding a needle in a haystack—a haystack that keeps getting bigger and a needle that keeps getting better at hiding.

U.S. imports from Mexico have doubled since the start of NAFTA in 1994, and most of this trade arrives via commercial cargo conveyances across the southwestern border. Commercial traffic from Mexico increased from 1.9 million arrivals in 1991 to more than 3.5 million in 1996. In Laredo, Texas, the busiest truck crossing point on the border, nearly one million trucks entered in 1997—up from 185,000 a decade earlier[113]—and the number is expected to double by 2010.

To avoid long delays, customs agents cannot realistically inspect most of the vehicles entering from Mexico.[114] The more intensive and intrusive the inspection process, the longer the wait at the border. The Customs Service, of course, must claim that "narcotics enforcement . . . comes first, even if trade facilitation suffers when counternarcotics operations slow the flow of commerce."[115] But although the domestic political context leads officials to declare their primary allegiance to border control, economic realities dictate that the border must remain highly porous; hence, prioritizing enforcement over facilitation is much easier said than done. As one senior customs official has explained, "If we examined every truck for narcotics arriving into the United States along the Southwest border. . . . Customs would back up the truck traffic bumper-to-bumper into Mexico City in just two weeks—15.8 days. In 15.8 days, there would be 95,608 trucks backed up into Mexico. That's 1,177 miles of trucks, end to end."[116]

Heightened political concern that free trade inadvertently aids drug smuggling has made border officials increasingly wary of projecting the impression that they are facilitating trade at the expense of enforcement. Indeed, some officials have erased the word "facilitation" from their vocabulary, opting instead to talk in terms of "traffic management." One senior customs official says that facilitation has become the "F word," sending the "wrong message" to Congress, the public, and the trade commu-

112. *New York Times,* 20 September 1998.

113. *New York Times,* 20 March 1998.

114. U.S. Customs Commissioner Samuel Banks has claimed that "over the last four years, we've gone from inspecting 5 percent of the trucks to 25 percent of the trucks" crossing the border. Quoted in *Journal of Commerce,* 16 March 1998.

115. U.S. Customs Service, *Enhanced Truck Inspection: Report to Congress* (Washington, D.C., September 1997), 5.

116. Remarks of Harvey G. Pothier, deputy assistant commissioner, Office of Air Interdiction, U.S. Customs Service, in Congressional Research Service, *Drug Interdiction,* 22.

nity.[117] Similarly, any evidence that the border has become easier to cross legally is handled with reassurances that the border is also being made more difficult to cross illegally. For example, the release of a study showing that traffic was moving more quickly through the San Ysidro port of entry south of San Diego (the busiest border crossing in the world) was purposely delayed until it could be shown that enforcement had also been beefed up.[118]

Yet despite these careful efforts to construct an image of heightened border security, the rising flow of commerce has provided an irresistible opportunity for political entrepreneurs to attack the administration as being "soft" on border control, and for bureaucratic entrepreneurs to deflect blame for policy failure and push for more enforcement resources.[119] Leading the political charge has been Senator Diane Feinstein (D-Calif.), who raised the border interdiction issue in the mid-1990s after press reports that the Customs Service was being lax on truck inspections in order to promote trade. In a 5 February 1996 letter to President Clinton, Feinstein blamed "customer-friendly" policies on the border for the influx of cocaine and even asked the president to replace George Weise, the commissioner of the Customs Service.[120]

What had drawn Feinstein's attention was the program called Line Release, which allowed customs agents to wave preapproved trucks through a port of entry without inspection. Criticizing the program for failing to run background checks on trucking companies and drivers, Feinstein called it "a superhighway for smugglers."[121] Although Line Release began in 1987, it did not attract much media and political attention until after the passage of NAFTA. In 1994, NAFTA's first year, 2.7 million Line Release vehicles crossed the border—a 44 percent increase over 1993.[122]

Free-trade opponents from both ends of the political spectrum have also opportunistically used the drug issue to bolster their positions. Patrick Buchanan, for example, has attacked both Republicans and Democrats

117. Author interview, U.S. Customs Service, San Diego, Calif., 4 April 1997.

118. Author interview, San Diego Dialogue, La Jolla, Calif., 12 May 1997. The San Diego Dialogue is a public policy center at the University of California at San Diego which publishes the "Border Wait Time Reports."

119. For example, Operation Alliance, which helps coordinate federal law enforcement efforts on the southwestern border, produced a May 1997 report on the negative consequences of NAFTA for drug control. The report was subsequently leaked to the press, generating prominent media coverage which, in turn, provided ammunition for key voices in Congress to push for beefed-up border controls.

120. *Washington Post,* 20 February 1996.

121. Quoted in Mike Allen, "Importers' Ire Up over Border Inspection Rise," *San Diego Business Journal,* 31 July 1995, pp. 1, 17.

122. *Narcotics Enforcement and Prevention Digest* 1, no. 10 (1995): 1.

for supporting NAFTA, which he says has made the border "wide open" to drug trafficking.[123] Three days before the congressional vote on whether to grant President Clinton fast-track authority to negotiate trade agreements, Representative Maxine Waters (D-Calif.) held a press conference to release a report titled *Drug Trafficking on the Fast Track*. The report urged that the Customs Service should be required to inspect 75 percent of all trucks and commercial maritime vessels at points of entry into the United States.[124] Such a sharp increase in the level of inspection is technically possible but realistically unthinkable; in practice, it would virtually shut down the border. The Nixon administration, it should be remembered, tried such intensive inspections for a few weeks during Operation Intercept in 1969. Today, as one customs official notes, it couldn't be done for even a few days because of the damage to trade.[125] Business leaders along the border already complain about the traffic jams and long delays, which they blame on stepped-up drug inspections.[126]

But even as increased cross-border economic integration has placed practical limitations on border controls, domestic political imperatives have necessitated that the administration devote ever more resources to the enhancement of such controls. The administration has attempted to counter political charges that it is facilitating too much and enforcing too little by increasing cargo inspections at the ports of entry. Thus, in February 1995 the Customs Service announced Operation Hard Line, an intensified effort to target drug smuggling in commercial cargo. Customs received 657 new positions through Hard Line in FY 1997—roughly a 25 percent increase in personnel on the border.[127]

Operation Hard Line provided a major boost to the San Diego sector in particular, which had been the focus of Senator Feinstein's attacks. Staffing for the San Diego office of Customs Investigations, for example, almost doubled between 1994 and 1996, including personnel moved to the San Diego sector from the interior.[128]

A year after Operation Hard Line was initiated, the Customs Service issued a press release praising the program's "record-breaking success": 24 percent more seizures of cocaine, heroin, and marijuana than in the previous year. Another press release a few days later boasted that the number of drug seizures along the California-Mexico border had increased by 76 percent over the same period the year before. The fine print, however,

123. Reuters, 22 June 1999.

124. Office of Representative Maxine Waters, *Drug Trafficking on the Fast Track: Executive Summary* (Washington, D.C., 4 November 1997).

125. Author interview, U.S. Customs Service, San Diego, Calif., 21 March 1997.

126. *San Antonio Express News,* 24 March 1999.

127. Author interview, U.S. Customs Service, Washington, D.C., 4 June 1997.

128. Author interview, U.S. Customs Service, San Diego, Calif., 21 March 1997.

revealed that although the overall number of drug seizures was up, the actual amount seized had fallen—suggesting that smugglers had adapted to the increased enforcement by breaking their loads into smaller packages to reduce their risks.[129] The trend has in fact been toward more but smaller drug shipments—creating more and harder work for customs. Inspectors spend most of their time overwhelmed with small-scale marijuana busts. Indeed, some officials believe smugglers use small marijuana shipments as a decoy to distract inspectors while they move larger and better hidden shipments through the ports of entry.

The Customs Service has also attributed a dramatic increase in arrests at the ports of entry to its efforts to harden the border. For example, the number of drug-related border arrests in southern California produced by customs investigations jumped from about 400 in 1992 to about 3,500 in 1996.[130] Such arrests have served the important political purpose of showing increased activity, even if not necessarily increased effectiveness. Those arrested have tended to be the most expendable and easily replaceable foot soldiers in the drug trade.[131] And the smugglers eliminated by increased arrests are some of the least skilled and sophisticated, many of whom specialize in marijuana (which is a bulkier product than cocaine, and easier to detect by drug-sniffing dogs).

U.S. officials have long acknowledged that seizures at the border ports of entry represent only a small percentage of the cross-border flow of drugs. Moreover, as the head of the U.S. Customs Service in San Diego has noted, traffickers assume that a certain percentage of their product will be seized and calculate this into their profit projections.[132] Nevertheless, seizure statistics are the leading instrument used by the Customs Service to justify its mission, fend off political attacks, and assure continued funding. In other words, there is a bureaucratic imperative to generate seizures in order to project a positive impression of enforcement effort—regardless of what these seizures actually mean. For example, when George Weise, customs commissioner, appeared on *Nightline* in May 1997 to defend his agency against charges of lax border inspections, he pointed to the substantial increase in drugs that had been seized in commercial cargo since Operation Hard Line was initiated—even though such an increase could simply indicate that concealment in commercial cargo was becoming an increasingly popular smuggling method.[133]

When cocaine seizure levels declined in 1997, customs officials predict-

129. Customs Service press releases, 26 and 28 February 1996.
130. Author interview, U.S. Customs Service, San Diego, Calif., 21 February 1997.
131. Author interview, U.S. Customs Service, San Diego, Calif., 7 April 1997.
132. Ibid.
133. ABC News, *Nightline,* 6 May 1997.

ably reacted with alarm. A 28 November 1997 National Treasury Employees Union memo noted that Congress had provided millions in new funding for enforcement positions for Operation Hard Line and warned that "no doubt Congress will be highly upset with these 1997 [seizure] figures . . . [because] border drug interdiction is becoming a major political issue in Washington." A similar memo on 22 December declared that new enforcement efforts were necessary, "the objective being to increase our seizures so customs and the union don't get their heads handed to them by the politicians in Washington when the budget meetings start in March."[134]

The low seizure levels did indeed provoke political grumbling. "Congress has directed almost every possible resource toward drug interdiction efforts, including more agents, better technology and several hundred million dollars in additional funding," said Representative Ron Packard (R-Calif.). "These are not the results we expected. If interdiction is down, the American people deserve some answers." In response, the Customs Service launched Operation Brass Ring in early 1998, which the commissioner promised would "dramatically increase drug seizures."[135]

To keep generating drug seizures without stopping the rising flow of commercial traffic, border control strategists have turned to state-of-the-art technologies. Alan Bersin, the attorney general's designated "border czar" until mid-1998, has explained the dilemma and its solution:

> Our border is intended to accomplish twin purposes; on the one hand, it is intended to facilitate trade in order to bring our nation the significant benefits of international commerce and industry. At the same time, it is geared to constrain and regulate the free movement of people and goods in order to block the entry of illegal migrants and unlawful merchandise. The key to resolving these apparently contradictory purposes lies in the strategic application of modern technology. We can and must have a border that is both secure and business-friendly.[136]

To help filter out illegal from legal flows, giant X-ray machines, large enough to drive a truck through, are being installed along the border. These machines, costing $3.5 million each, are expected to be in place at all thirty-nine border ports of entry by the year 2003.[137] (In response, smugglers are reportedly already developing compartments that are im-

134. Quoted in *Los Angeles Times,* 4 February 1998.
135. Quoted in ibid.
136. Testimony of Alan D. Bersin, U.S. attorney for the Southern District of California, House Appropriations Subcommittee of the Departments of Commerce, Justice, and State, the Judiciary and Related Agencies, *Departments of Commerce, Justice, and State, The Judiciary and Related Agencies Appropriations for 1996,* 104th Cong., 1st sess., 29 March 1995.
137. *San Francisco Examiner,* 31 August 1998.

pervious to X-rays.) [138] Also being adapted to border law enforcement is equipment previously restricted to military use in the Cold War era. In March 1995 a Border Research Technology Center was opened in San Diego for this purpose.[139] Experimental devices tested include an electronic current that disables a fleeing car and an ion scanner designed to detect drugs hidden in vehicles.[140]

The intense political fire directed at border inspectors for not doing more to reduce the flow of drugs has translated into increased political support for more resources to harden the ports of entry. "Our borders are being overrun by drug dealers," Senator Phil Gramm (R-Tex.) has warned.[141] His proposed solution: hire 1,000 new Customs Service inspectors and devote $56 million to technological improvements, including surveillance cameras, mobile and stationary X-ray machines to inspect trucks, and ultrasonic machines to scan containers. A spokesperson for Senator Gramm justified these requests by stating, "We need to do what's necessary to increase the legal trade and shut off the flow of illegal drugs." Making that happen, he said, will "take a great deal more equipment and people."[142]

The White House has been an especially enthusiastic advocate of a high-tech solution to the dilemmas of drug interdiction in the age of NAFTA.[143] As the drug policy director Barry McCaffrey has put it, "Technology can help us stop drugs while facilitating legal commerce."[144] In September 1998 he told a congressional committee that we cannot deter drugs "unless we give the Customs Service and the Border Patrol the tools they need to do their job. That's where we need congressional focus and resources." We can "fix" the border, he asserted: "It is achievable. We can use high-technology, non-intrusive inspection systems, linked intelligence, change manpower and doctrine to protect the American people along the

138. Testimony of Samuel H. Banks, deputy commissioner of Customs, House Subcommittee on Criminal Justice, Drug Policy, and Human Resources, Government Reform Committee, *Examining the Drug Threat Along the Southwest Border*, 106th Cong., 1st sess., 24 September, 1999.

139. The technology center receives its funding from the National Institute of Justice. The Office of National Drug Control Policy also has a counterdrug technology assessment center. The Customs Service, however, remains the primary developer of technology for the detection of contraband. Author interview with Chris Aldridge, Border Research and Technology Center, San Diego, Calif., 7 March 1997.

140. *San Diego Union-Tribune*, 18 March 1995.

141. Quoted in *Arizona Daily Star*, 4 June 1999.

142. Quoted in *Houston Chronicle*, 4 January 1998.

143. See Office of National Drug Control Policy, *Ten Year Counterdrug Technology Plan and Development Roadmap* (Washington, D.C., February 1999).

144. Testimony of Barry R. McCaffrey, House Subcommittee on Criminal Justice, Drug Policy, and Human Resources, Government Reform and Oversight Committee, 106th Cong., 1st sess., 25 February 1999.

Southwest border."[145] And so the buildup of border drug enforcement continues, but in an increasingly high-tech fashion.

THE POLITICS OF MEASURING POLICY EFFECTIVENESS

However forcefully government officials promote a bigger and better border interdiction campaign, the built-in limits of such a deterrence effort have long been known. In 1993 the Government Accounting Office (GAO), the investigative arm of Congress, reported that "interdiction has not had—and is unlikely to have—a significant impact on the national goal of reducing drug supplies to the United States. The enormous profits in cocaine make interdiction losses relatively inconsequential."[146]

Even unimaginable interdiction successes would not significantly affect drug prices on the street because most of the value added (roughly 90 percent of the street price in the case of cocaine) is imposed after the product crosses the border (reflecting the risks and costs imposed by domestic law enforcement). Since the cost of the drug before it enters the country represents only a small percentage of the retail price, smugglers can easily replace lost loads.[147]

Yet when the instrumental value of the interdiction campaign is challenged by evidence that it is an inherently inefficient enforcement tool, officials take refuge in its symbolic value—and dismiss anyone who disregards it. In response to "those who argue that interdiction is a hopeless endeavor," the Bush White House insisted that "a civilized society does not leave its border totally open to those who would harm its citizens. Interdiction has both symbolic and real value. It demonstrates our national will to oppose drug traffickers on every available front."[148] Thus, largely on the basis of its symbolic merits, border interdiction has become not simply a means to an end (reducing the drug supply) but an end in itself.

Part of the political and bureaucratic allure of interdiction is that it gen-

145. Testimony of Barry R. McCaffrey before the Senate Foreign Relations Committee and the Caucus on International Narcotics Control, *The Western Hemisphere Drug Elimination Act*, 105th Cong., 2d sess., 16 September 1998.

146. Testimony of Louis J. Rodrigues, director, Systems Development and Production Issues, National Security and International Affairs Division, Senate Subcommittee on Treasury, Postal Service, and General Government, Committee on Appropriations, *Border Drug Interdiction*, 103d Cong., 1st sess., 25 February 1993, 148.

147. See Peter Reuter, Gordon Crawford, and Jonathan Cave, *Sealing the Borders* (Santa Monica, Calif.: RAND Corporation, 1988). Also see Peter Reuter, "Quantity Illusions and Paradoxes of Drug Interdiction: Federal Investigation into Vice Policy," *Law and Contemporary Problems* 51, no. 1 (1988): 232–52.

148. Office of National Drug Control Policy, *National Drug Control Strategy* (Washington, D.C., 1991), 94.

erates indicators of government resolve that are perceptually appealing even if highly misleading. Senator John McCain has explained in blunt terms that

> it is easy to talk of a war on drugs, involve our military in an antidrug program, pour billions into the effort, and then disguise a lack of success with reassuring rhetoric. . . . The measures of success that are being made public have virtually no practical meaning. For example, efforts to assist seizures are measured in terms of the amount of drugs seized, with no effort to relate such data to the percentage of total drugs that get through, or to whether seizures have any meaningful impact on the main smuggling networks. . . . Another equally meaningless measure of capability is to report the number of detections, arrests, or intercepts, with no attempt to relate this to the number of successful crossings or actual convictions, or whether such actions have any real effect on the flow of drugs.[149]

Distorted evaluations and the use of partial indicators of effectiveness are certainly not new. In 1973 the National Commission on Marijuana and Drug Abuse pointed out that the drug control

> funding mechanism is so structured that it responds only when "bodies" can be produced or counted. Such a structure penalizes a reduction in the body count, while it rewards any increase in incidence figures and arrest statistics with more money. Those receiving funds have a vested interest in increasing or maintaining those figures. The statistics, in turn, fuel public and bureaucratic concerns, and assure that the problem continues to be defined incorrectly.

These kinds of figures, concluded the commission, "are dramatic, but do not really tell what is happening." Increased numbers of arrests, for instance, "may simply mean more violators, rather than more effective enforcement." Similarly, "the quantities of drugs seized may reflect only the size of the illegal market."[150]

More than a quarter-century later the reliance on misleading measures of effectiveness persists, but the political stage on which they are displayed has significantly expanded. In 1972 only two Senate committees and one House committee held hearings on proposed drug legislation; by the mid-1980s, drug policy cut across the jurisdiction of some seventy-four congressional committees and subcommittees. Consequently, congressional hearings have become an increasingly important forum for evaluating and

149. Quoted in J. F. Holden-Rhodes, *Sharing the Secrets: Open Source Intelligence and the War on Drugs* (Westport, Conn.: Praeger, 1997), 190.

150. National Commission on Marihuana and Drug Abuse, *Drug Use in America: Problem in Perspective, Second Report* (Washington, D.C., 1973), 282, 227.

promoting the federal antidrug effort. Each hearing follows the same basic routine: the chair delivers an opening statement about the scourge of drugs, insisting that we must do more to stop drugs from crossing the nation's borders. Other committee members then offer their own variations on the same theme. These are followed by testimonies from drug enforcement officials, highlighting what their agencies have accomplished and what they hope to accomplish if more resources are forthcoming from Congress.

Each agency is concerned only about showing the success of its discrete mission, rather than with the viability of the policy as a whole. Each has its own way of measuring and justifying its performance: for example, the Customs Service highlights seizures and arrests at the border ports of entry; the DEA prioritizes the capture of major traffickers; the State Department stresses the level of cooperation with Mexico. Poor results tend to be blamed on mismanagement and insufficient resources. Improved results are assumed to come from more and better law enforcement and cross-border cooperation. The question-and-answer period that follows the prepared official testimonies can often be heated, but given the political and bureaucratic interests involved, there is rarely any challenge to the basic underlying supply-side logic of the drug control strategy.

Projecting an impression of cross-border commitment and progress in the antidrug campaign has ultimately proved to be more politically consequential for U.S. and Mexican leaders than whether or not the drug supply has actually been reduced. Regardless of its deterrent effect, the escalation of enforcement efforts has helped to fend off political attacks and kept the drug issue from derailing the broader process of economic integration. In other words, a policy that has largely failed in its stated goal has nevertheless helped to realize other key political objectives—most notably the creation and maintenance of NAFTA. The intensified antidrug campaign, however, has brought with it significant collateral damage: more corruption, more militarized law enforcement, more linkages between the drug trade and legitimate cross-border trade, and a generally more "narcoticized" U.S.-Mexico relationship.

CHAPTER FIVE

The Escalation of Immigration Control

Efforts to police the flow of illegal immigrants across the U.S.-Mexico border have undergone a metamorphosis since the early 1990s: immigration control along the border has been elevated from one of the most neglected areas of federal law enforcement to one of the most politically popular. The unprecedented expansion of border policing, I argue, has ultimately been less about achieving the stated instrumental goal of deterring illegal border crossers and more about politically recrafting the image of the border and symbolically reaffirming the state's territorial authority. Although the escalation of policing has largely failed as a deterrent and has generated perverse and counterproductive consequences that reinforce calls for further escalation, it has been strikingly successful in projecting the appearance of a more secure and orderly border.

The escalation of border enforcement has influenced where, how, and how often illegal immigrants cross the border. This has generated enormous rewards for lawmakers, law enforcers, and law-evading migrant smugglers and has powerfully shaped public and media perception. At the same time, the narrow and symbolically appealing focus on the borderline itself as both the source of the illegal immigration problem and the site of the policing solution has drawn attention away from the more politically awkward and divisive task of formally recognizing and regulating a well-entrenched clandestine cross-border labor market.

CREATING AND CHANNELING THE BACKLASH AGAINST ILLEGAL IMMIGRATION

During much of the twentieth century, the United States and Mexico not only quietly tolerated but actively facilitated and encouraged the influx of cheap labor across the border; until recent decades the rising level of illegal immigration commanded little national political attention. For example, the platform of the Republican Party did not even mention immigration control until 1980, and only four years later did it affirm the country's right to control its borders and express concern about illegal immigration.[1]

Congressional debate over how to deal with illegal immigration culminated in the passage of the Immigration Reform and Control Act of 1986, which introduced employer sanctions for the first time, as well as a limited legalization program. But although IRCA provided a temporary sedative, the law exacerbated the very problem it purported to remedy. Rather than discouraging illegal immigration, the main impact of legalization under IRCA was to reinforce and expand already well-established cross-border migration networks. Many onetime immigrants who had gone back to Mexico returned to claim legalization papers. And those who were legalized under the program provided a more secure base for the arrival of new immigrants. Meanwhile, the primary impact of the poorly designed and minimally enforced employer sanctions was to create a booming business in fraudulent documents.

IRCA's perverse consequences helped set the stage for a powerful backlash against illegal immigration in the 1990s, most acute in California, which was home to nearly half of the unauthorized immigrants estimated to be in the country. The state was hit hard early in the decade by a budget crisis and an economic downturn occasioned by post–Cold War cuts in military support for southern California's aerospace industry. Economic insecurity combined with a rapidly changing demographic profile to nurture rising nativist fears among California's disproportionately white, middle-class electorate. The new restrictionist mood was embodied in the passage of Proposition 187 by California voters in 1994, which sought to bar illegal immigrants from receiving social services. Proposition 187 was self-consciously designed and promoted as a symbolic gesture to express frustration and "send a message" to the federal government.[2] Even though it was subsequently declared unconstitutional (as its proponents expected), its passage by a three-to-two margin sent shock waves across the country and through the halls of Congress.

My purpose is not to provide a general explanation for the anti–illegal immigration backlash but, more specifically, to show how this backlash was partly created and then opportunistically channeled by political and bu-

1. Joseph Nevins, "'Illegal Aliens' and the Political Geography of Criminalized Immigrants" (paper presented at the annual meeting of the Association of American Geographers, Boston, 28 March 1998).

2. Kitty Calavita, "The New Politics of Immigration: 'Balanced-Budget Conservatism' and the Symbolism of Proposition 187," *Social Problems* 43, no. 3 (1996): 284–305.

reaucratic entrepreneurs to focus on the border as both the source of the problem and the most appropriate site of the policy solution. Beginning with Patrick Buchanan, politicians used the border as a political prop in voicing their opposition to illegal immigration. During the 1992 presidential campaign Buchanan held a press conference above Smugglers Canyon (a well-known point of illegal entry along the border south of San Diego) to denounce what he called the federal government's failure to deter an "illegal invasion." In the following years more mainstream politicians embraced many of Buchanan's ideas and similarly adopted the border as a political stage.[3]

In a brilliant political move, Governor Pete Wilson of California revived his floundering 1994 electoral campaign by blaming the state's woes on the federal government's failure to control the border. His most effective tool for communicating this message was a television advertisement based on video footage of illegal immigrants dashing across the border from Mexico into the southbound traffic at the San Ysidro port of entry. Against the background of this chaotic scene the narrator's voice said: "They keep coming. Two million illegal immigrants in California. The federal government won't stop them at the border, yet requires us to pay billions to take care of them. Governor Wilson sent the National Guard to help the Border Patrol. But that's not all." Governor Wilson then appeared, pledging to do more: "For Californians who work hard, pay taxes and obey the laws, I am suing to force the federal government to control the border and I'm working to deny state services to illegal immigrants. Enough is enough."[4] Only a few years earlier, it should be recalled, Wilson had asked for a relaxation of controls so that Mexican workers could cross the border to apply for special agricultural workers' visas.

Far from being passive bystanders, border officials helped construct this image of the border under siege. Not only did the Border Patrol produce the original video footage used in the Wilson campaign;[5] it helped to create the spectacle of an overrun port of entry in the first place. While the Wilson ad conveyed the impression that this disorderly scene was an everyday occurrence, it had in fact been sparked in 1992 by intensified Border Patrol pressure on illegal crossers to the west of the port of entry.[6] Squeezed by the deployment of more agents and a new fence along the

3. Sebastian Rotella, *Twilight on the Line: Underworlds and Politics at the U.S.-Mexico Border* (New York: Norton, 1998), 30.

4. Quoted in Katrina Burgess and Carlos González Gutierrez, "Reluctant Partner: California in U.S.-Mexico Relations" (unpublished manuscript, n.d.), 29–30.

5. Author interview, Border Patrol Western Regional Headquarters, Laguna Niguel, Calif., 27 March 1997.

6. Author interview with Douglas Kruhm, former Assistant Commissioner of the Border Patrol, Washington, D.C., 6 February 1998.

westernmost five-mile stretch of the border[7] (traditionally the single most heavily used point for illegal entry), smugglers responded by orchestrating charges of fifty migrants at a time—called "Banzai runs" by border officials—through the southbound lanes of the San Ysidro port of entry.

The dramatic footage of men, women, and children dashing across the border and weaving through the busy traffic was broadcast across the nation, providing a powerful focusing event that galvanized public attention. Critics accused the Border Patrol of deliberately provoking the charges and playing up the images to secure more funding.[8] The scenes of the Banzai runs were not only exploited for political gain by Governor Wilson[9] but projected the message that lax border controls were the root of the illegal immigration problem. Left out of this message was the anemic condition of workplace controls, the economic reliance of key sectors of the California economy (particularly agriculture) on illegal foreign workers, and the fact that 40–50 percent of the unauthorized immigrants in the country had not entered illegally but simply overstayed their visas.

Instead of challenging this border-focused message, both Republicans and Democrats embraced it. Targeting the border (rather than, say, domestic employer demand for inexpensive labor) not only had an irresistible symbolic appeal but helped define the nature of the problem and limited the range of acceptable policy solutions. To a remarkable extent, then, official policy debate over illegal immigration was quickly reduced to a narrow debate over controlling the border. Politicians across the political spectrum sounded increasingly alike in pledging their commitment to border control. For example, echoing popular political sentiment, Representative Brian Bilbray (R-Calif.) exclaimed that "We have traveled all over the world as a nation since 1914, securing the frontiers of other nations, but the greatest power in the world has not chosen to secure its own national territory."[10] And as President Clinton put it, "We can't afford to lose control of our own borders at a time when we are not adequately providing for the jobs, health care, and the education of our own people."[11] Hav-

7. Built by the military, the fence was funded and justified as a deterrent against drug smugglers driving loads across the border. Although in practice it served immigration control purposes as well, it had to be built as a drug-control fence in order to secure military assistance and minimize political opposition to the idea: ibid.

8. Rotella, *Twilight on the Line,* 55.

9. As Alan D. Bersin, the U.S. attorney for the Southern District of California (appointed by Janet Reno as the administration's point person on border issues), put it, "the Banzai runners re-elected Pete Wilson": speech at the Institute of the Americas, University of California, San Diego, La Jolla, Calif., 11 July 1997.

10. House Subcommittee on Immigration and Claims, Committee on the Judiciary, *Border Security: Hearing before the Subcommittee on Immigration and Claims of the Committee on the Judiciary,* 104th Cong., 1st sess., 10 March 1995, 6.

11. ABC News, *This Week with David Brinkley,* 20 June 1993.

ing identified the border as the political battleground on which the government's resolve to fight illegal immigration would be tested, politicians rushed to outdo one another in proposing tough new measures.

THE U.S. BORDER CONTROL OFFENSIVE

Although border control was a low priority for President Clinton when he first took office, he soon became an enthusiastic proponent of tighter controls in order keep up with Republican initiatives in Congress. In late July 1993 he held a news conference to announce aggressive new measures against illegal immigration: "Today we send a strong and clear message. We will make it tougher for illegal aliens to get into our country." These measures included hiring 600 more Border Patrol agents—an idea Clinton adopted as his own, though the proposal actually came from an amendment proposed earlier in the month by Representative Duncan Hunter (R-Calif.). In announcing the increase, the President said, "It's certainly plain to anybody with eyes to see that the Border Patrol is drastically understaffed, breathtakingly understaffed." (Just a few months earlier he had actually recommended trimming its size as a cost-saving measure.) [12] Signaling the administration's new commitment, the attorney general and the INS commissioner became frequent visitors to the border. [13] The attorney general even appointed a Special Representative to the Southwest Border (who was immediately dubbed the "border czar" by the press). Officials of the Border Patrol (the uniformed enforcement wing of the INS), long accustomed to being outside the political spotlight and marginalized within the criminal justice system, were suddenly brought center stage—and indeed were even invited for the first time to the White House for press announcements with the president. [14]

The heightened status of immigration control has been reflected in the unprecedented expansion of the INS. Long viewed as the neglected stepchild of the Department of Justice, it has become one of the fastest growing federal agencies. The INS budget nearly tripled between FY 1993 and 1999, from $1.5 billion to $4.2 billion, and the single most important growth area has been border enforcement. Between 1994 and 1998 more than $3.3 billion was spent on the Border Patrol, whose own annual budget jumped from $354 million in 1993 to $877 million in 1998—a 148 percent increase.

12. Quoted in Fred Barnes, "No Entry: The Republicans' Immigration War," *New Republic,* 8 November 1993, 10–13.

13. Attorney General Janet Reno made fourteen trips to San Diego alone between 1994 and 1998: *Los Angeles Times,* 28 June 1998.

14. Author interview with Douglas Kruhm.

With much of the spending going toward hiring new agents, the INS now has more officers authorized to carry a gun and make arrests than any other federal agency. From 1993 to October 1999 the number of Border Patrol agents in the Southwest more than doubled, from 3,389 to some 8,200. In the San Diego sector alone the number rose from 998 in October 1994 to 2,264 by June 1998, and there are as many agents in this sector as there were along the entire southwestern border in the 1970s.[15] The infusion of personnel has been matched by new fencing, equipment, and surveillance devices: infrared night-vision scopes, low-light TV cameras, ground sensors, helicopters, and all-terrain vehicles.[16] To "thicken" the border, the Border Patrol has also expanded its checkpoints on the roads leading north.

The rapid growth of the INS is particularly impressive because it has taken place in an era otherwise characterized by government downsizing. While most federal agencies have been struggling in the face of budget cuts, the INS has been struggling to manage its fast-paced expansion. The positions of "Border Patrol Agent" and "Immigration Inspector" have been listed as two of the top ten areas of job growth in the federal government.[17] The INS has established an around-the-clock hotline for prospective applicants, hired an advertising agency, expanded its recruitment at colleges, military bases, and job fairs, and begun promoting its careers on the Internet.[18] Thus, although "devolution" (less federal spending and more responsibility transferred to state governments) has been a popular political theme, current trends in immigration control push in the opposite direction.

The border buildup is scheduled to continue at a fast pace. The Illegal Immigration Reform and Immigration Responsibility Act of 1996 calls for hiring 1,000 new Border Patrol agents a year and a total force of 10,000 by the year 2001. All new recruits are sent to the southwestern border where over 90 percent of the Border Patrol is deployed.[19] Among other measures,

15. Author interview, U.S. Border Patrol, San Diego Sector Headquarters, San Diego, Calif., 4 March 1997.

16. Between October 1994 and June 1998 the number of infrared scopes in the San Diego sector increased from 12 to 599; underground sensors from 448 to 1,214; computers from 100 to more than 1,350; and vehicles from 700 to more than 1,765: *INS Fact Sheet,* 14 July 1998.

17. Leigh Rivenbark, "Help Wanted," *Federal Times,* 28 July 1997, 1, 14.

18. *Washington Post,* 13 May 1999. The Border Patrol has also used mass E-mail within the Justice Department to recruit new applicants. A sample that was diverted my way targeted federal employees living in cold climates with the allure of a posting along the sunny and warm southern border.

19. Associated Press, 4 January 2000.

the act promotes tougher sentencing guidelines: mandatory minimum sentencing for those convicted of smuggling aliens for commercial gain and, in some cases, a doubling of penalties. The 1996 law also authorizes the construction of new physical barriers, most notably a multilayered fence to reinforce the fourteen miles of fencing already in place south of San Diego. (In the San Diego sector the length of border fencing has more than doubled since 1994.) The extra fencing was first recommended by a study prepared by Sandia Laboratories, a national weapons lab. Arguing that "the illegal aliens have shown that they will destroy or bypass any single measure placed in their path," the Sandia study concluded that "a three-fence barrier system with vehicle patrol roads between the fences and lights will provide the necessary discouragement."[20] The biggest advocate of the new fencing, Representative Duncan Hunter (R-Calif.), has proposed building a similar barrier system at each of the major urban corridors along the southwestern border. The second fourteen-mile layer of fencing south of San Diego will cost $25 million and is expected to be completed in 2001.[21]

The military too has played an important support role on the border. Praising the growing cooperation and coordination between law enforcement and the military, INS Commissioner Doris Meissner has said, "Think of this as one team, different roles, different uniforms, but with the same game plan—and that is to restore the rule of law to the border."[22] Although prohibited from making arrests, military personnel do assist the INS by operating night scopes, motion sensors, and communications equipment and by building and maintaining roads and fences. South of San Diego it was army reservists who constructed a ten-foot-high steel fence. In Nogales, Arizona, army engineers installed a fifteen-foot fence nearly five miles long, extending from one end of town to the other. New fencing is also going up elsewhere along the border.

Technologies and equipment originally developed for military use have increasingly been adapted for border enforcement purposes. Magnetic footfall detectors and infrared body sensors, many of which were first used in Vietnam, are deployed along the border. An electronic finger-printing system (called IDENT), adapted from the Navy's Deployable Mass Population Identification and Tracking System, is used by the Border Patrol to keep records on apprehended border crossers. The Border Research and Technology Center established in San Diego continues to facilitate the

20. Sandia National Laboratories, *Systematic Analysis of the Southwest Border* (report prepared for the INS, Washington, D.C., January 1993), ES-5.
21. *San Diego Union-Tribune,* 15 December 1999.
22. Doris Meissner and Janet Reno news conference, 12 January 1996.

conversion of defense technologies. Experimental devices tested include an electronic current that stops a fleeing car, a camera that can see into vehicles to find hidden passengers, and a computer that checks commuters by voiceprint.[23]

The administration's border control offensive is based on a strategy developed by the INS in 1993–94 called "prevention through deterrence."[24] The objective of increased fencing, surveillance equipment, penalties, and law enforcement personnel is to inhibit illegal entry and thus avoid having to apprehend entrants after they've crossed the border. Massive injections of law enforcement resources at the most popular points of unauthorized entry are designed to disrupt the human traffic, forcing migrants to attempt the crossing in more difficult, remote areas or at official ports of entry (which, the INS says are easier to control). The result, U.S. border control strategists argue, is that many would-be border crossers are discouraged from trying, and those who do try fail repeatedly and eventually give up because of frustration and depleted resources.

Such a strategy was first tested with the launching of Operation Blockade (later given the more diplomatic name of Hold-the-Line) in El Paso in September 1993. Silvestre Reyes, the El Paso Border Patrol chief who was the architect of the plan, faced initial resistance from his superiors at INS headquarters. There was concern that such a concentrated deployment of force would lead to violent confrontations and strain U.S. relations with Mexico on the eve of NAFTA. Moreover, the emphasis on deterring entry rather than apprehending migrants as they crossed contradicted the Border Patrol's traditional reliance on high apprehension numbers to justify budget requests.[25] Nevertheless, an enabling political climate and his own bureaucratic entrepreneurialism made it possible for Reyes to secure the overtime pay he needed to deploy 450 agents for intensive coverage of a twenty-mile stretch of the border.

As hoped, the operation led to a sharp drop in attempted entries in the El Paso sector. Previously, there had been up to 10,000 illegal border crossers per day, and only one of eight had been apprehended.[26] The high-profile show of force quickly reduced this flow to a trickle, drawing the immediate attention of Washington, the media, and California politicians

23. *San Diego Union-Tribune*, 18 March 1995.

24. *Border Patrol Strategic Plan 1994 and Beyond: National Strategy* (Washington, D.C.: U.S. Border Patrol, July 1994).

25. Author interview with Representative Silvestre Reyes (D-Tex.), former El Paso Border Patrol chief, Washington, D.C., 4 February 1998.

26. Testimony of Laurie E. Ekstrand, U.S. General Accounting Office, House Subcommittee on Immigration and Claims, Committee on the Judiciary, *Border Security*, 104th Cong., 1st sess., 10 March 1995, 105–10.

eager to replicate the El Paso experience.[27] Bureaucratic resistance at the INS soon withered away as the operation was widely praised.[28] Chief Reyes became an overnight hero, and would later even be elected to Congress. The powerful appeal of Operation Hold-the-Line was that the results were both immediate and highly visible. Once it had achieved national attention, the INS had little choice but to promote it and take credit for its success.[29] One consequence was that the rewards system within the Border Patrol was suddenly turned upside down, prevention rather than number of apprehensions becoming the new enforcement goal.

In consultation with the Defense Department's Center for Low Intensity Conflict, in 1994 the INS developed a comprehensive plan to apply "prevention through deterrence" across the rest of the border. The strategy would first focus on the busiest points of illegal entry: the El Paso and San Diego sectors, which in FY 1993 had accounted for 68 percent of all apprehensions. Thus, in October 1994, El Paso's Operation Hold-the-Line was joined by Operation Gatekeeper south of San Diego, which targeted the fourteen westernmost miles of the border. Together, these two operations covered the border areas that had traditionally accounted for two-thirds or more of all illegal entries. The plan was then to extend the strategy to the Tucson sector and south Texas—to which migrants were expected to turn after the El Paso and San Diego sectors were secured—and ultimately to the entire boundary. The vision was the restoration of the country's "confidence in the integrity of the border."[30]

SELF-PERPETUATING ESCALATION

An enabling political climate and bureaucratic entrepreneurialism helped launch the new border control offensive, but once initiated, it became self-reinforcing. The tightening of controls in El Paso and San Diego predictably pushed migrants to attempt entry elsewhere; consequently, apprehensions remain far below previous levels in the El Paso sector but have jumped in New Mexico and Arizona. Similarly, apprehensions in the Imperial Beach sector south of San Diego have declined sharply since Gatekeeper began, but arrests have skyrocketed in the remote parts of eastern San Diego County.

27. Apprehensions in the El Paso sector dropped 72 percent from FY 1993 to 1994: ibid.
28. According to an El Paso poll of February 1994, 84 percent favored the new Border Patrol strategy: ibid.
29. Author interview with Silvestre Reyes.
30. *Border Patrol Strategic Plan 1994 and Beyond*, 2.

These enforcement-induced shifts in the human traffic, dispersing the illegal migration flow from the traditional urban entry points, created a border version of NIMBY ("not in my back yard"). As crackdowns in one area pushed migrants to neighboring areas, officials and residents in those areas predictably lobbied for more Border Patrol agents and resources. Thus, Operation Safeguard was launched in Nogales, Arizona, in 1995 (and expanded to Douglas and Naco in 1999); Operation Gatekeeper was extended in October 1996 to cover sixty-six miles; and in January 1997 Operation Hold-the-Line was extended ten miles west into New Mexico. In late August 1997 the INS announced Operation Río Grande in southeast Texas, where it set up floodlights, twenty-foot watch towers, video cameras, and high-powered infrared vision scopes for thirty-one miles along the river.

As small border towns suddenly became major corridors of illegal crossings, new agents poured in and new fencing projects began. For example, in Douglas, Arizona, a new five-mile steel fence has been built (backed by a trench originally dug to deter Pancho Villa's army from crossing into the town during the Mexican Revolution), and the number of Border Patrol agents has increased fivefold since October 1994.[31] Apprehensions in this town of 15,000 residents have dramatically increased from 3,000 a month in 1995 to 27,000 in March 1999 alone.[32] The mayor of Douglas has complained that the stepped-up enforcement is "making our town a militarized zone."[33]

Similarly, in Naco, Arizona (population 7,000), the Border Patrol detained 1,600 illegal entrants annually a decade ago. In 1999, apprehensions passed this number by 1,000—in just the first twelve days of February.[34] Mexican towns across the Arizona border have boomed as a result of the influx of people heading north. Agua Prieta, for example, had six small hotels and 60,000 residents in the mid-1990s. By mid-1999 it was reported to have a population of 120,000, sixteen hotels, and numerous safe houses from which one hundred smugglers operate. Its central plaza had become a waiting place for some 3,000 people planning to cross the border, and the Border Patrol was returning an average of 20,000 apprehended Mexicans a month to the city.[35] "This people-smuggling business has surpassed narco-trafficking here," says Agua Prieta's mayor. "And the Border Patrol strategy is the reason."[36]

31. *Boston Globe,* 14 May 1998.
32. *Dallas Morning News,* 13 June 1999.
33. Quoted in *Arizona Republic,* 8 October 1999.
34. *Arizona Daily Star,* 14 February 1999.
35. *Migration News,* June 1999.
36. Quoted in *Arizona Daily Star,* 11 July 1999. The enforcement buildup along the Arizona-Mexico border in 1994–99 included an increase in Border Patrol agents from 287

The expanding Border Patrol presence in areas between the ports of entry, meanwhile, has sparked a surge in attempted illegal entries through the ports of entry themselves, and the INS has responded with an infusion of new port inspectors. Their number rose from 1,117 to 1,865 between FY 1994 and 1997, representing a 67 percent increase. At some crossing points, such as Calexico and San Ysidro in California, the number of inspectors has more than doubled. The vast majority of INS port-of-entry inspectors for the entire country are now assigned to the southwestern border. The increase in staffing has been matched by stiffer penalties: those who attempt entry through the fraudulent use of documents are being prosecuted for repeat violations, and vehicles may also be confiscated. In addition, to inhibit the use of forged documents, officials are moving to replace the old border-crossing cards with high-tech visas containing a digital fingerprint.

By disrupting the traditional routes and methods of clandestine entry, the intensified border control campaign has transformed the once relatively simple illegal act of crossing the border into a more complex system of illegal practices. Past forms of unauthorized entry primarily involved either self-smuggling or limited use of a local "coyote." With the escalation of border policing in recent years, however, the use of a professional smuggler has become standard practice. Indeed, as the Border Patrol chief of the San Diego Sector has put it, the whole border-crossing experience has been transformed into a smuggling game.[37] The increased use of smugglers, a 1997 report of the Binational Study on Migration concluded, "helps to explain why most migrants attempting unauthorized entry succeed despite significantly more U.S. Border Patrol agents and technology on the border."[38] The study's surveys found that nearly 75 percent of all illegal Mexican border crossers now use the services of a smuggler.

As the demand for smuggling services and the risks of crossing the border have gone up, so too has the price of being smuggled. Fees have jumped in some places from $250 per person to as much as $1,500.[39] Border control officials view the increases as a key sign that the policy is working. Yet higher prices are not necessarily a significant deterrent, given that much or all of the smuggling fee tends to be covered by relatives and

---

to 1,285, more than a doubling of underground sensors, a tripling of vehicles, and a quadrupling of the number of low-light TV cameras and night scopes: *INS Fact Sheet*, 8 October 1999.

37. Author interview, San Diego Border Patrol sector, San Diego, Calif., 4 March 1997.

38. See Binational Study on Migration, *Binational Study: Migration between Mexico and the United States* (Mexico City and Washington, D.C.: Mexican Foreign Ministry and U.S. Commission on Immigration Reform, 1997), 28. The study was a lengthy research project commissioned jointly by the U.S. and Mexican governments.

39. INS Fact Sheet, *INS' Southwest Border Strategy*, 1 May 1999.

friends already in the United States rather than by the immigrants themselves. The main impact of higher fees, it seems, has been to enrich increasingly sophisticated and well-organized binational smuggling groups. As Miguel Vallina, the assistant Border Patrol chief in San Diego has pointed out, "The more difficult the crossing, the better the business for the smugglers."[40] INS Commissioner Doris Meissner explained in January 1996 that "As we improve our enforcement, we increase the smuggling of aliens that occurs, because it is harder to cross and so therefore people turn more and more to smugglers."[41] But even as Meissner recognized that the Border Patrol creates business for smugglers, she also has said that "[we are] moving as aggressively as we can . . . so that we can put them [the smugglers] out of business."[42] Thus there is, on the one hand, a recognition that more enforcement fuels more smuggling but, on the other hand, an assurance that more enforcement will somehow end smuggling.

In practice, more enforcement has certainly put some smugglers out of business, but this has simply created business for their competitors: one smuggler's loss is another's gain. Smugglers are, at core, travel service specialists (even if sometimes abusive ones). And as long as there is a strong demand for their services (which the tightening of border controls guarantees), smuggling will likely persist. The high profits of the business, which have sharply increased since the border crackdown, assures that there will be smugglers willing to accept the occupational risks. As one smuggler working the border has explained, "Figure it this way. If I work in a factory five days, I make $125 a week. If I take one person across the border, I get $300."[43] A good guide can reportedly make $60,000 a year on the border.[44]

As border controls have improved, so too has the skill of smugglers in circumventing them. A senior INS official acknowledges, "Alien smugglers have developed a sophisticated infrastructure to successfully counteract U.S. Border Patrol operations."[45] A federal prosecutor agrees that the skill and sophistication of the smugglers have "improved dramatically."[46] The

40. Quoted in *Los Angeles Times,* 5 February 1995.

41. Janet Reno and Doris Meissner news conference.

42. Testimony of Doris Meissner, House Subcommittee on Commerce, Justice, State, and Judiciary, Appropriations Committee, *FY 97 Justice Appropriations,* 104th Cong., 2d sess., 8 May 1996.

43. Quoted in *Los Angeles Times,* 2 May 1992.

44. *San Diego Union-Tribune,* 28 April 1996.

45. Testimony of George Regan, INS acting associate commissioner of enforcement, House Subcommittee on Immigration and Claims, Committee on the Judiciary, *Combatting Illegal Immigration: A Progress Report,* 105th Cong., 1st sess., 23 April 1997.

46. Author interview, Office of the U.S. Attorney for the Southern District of California, San Diego, Calif., 1 April 1997.

operations that have the greatest transportation and communication capabilities are those most capable of evading law enforcement's tightening net. Some smugglers have literally gone underground, tunneling under the border defenses.[47] Others have turned to transporting migrants in 18-wheelers that blend in with the boom in cross-border trucking brought on by the liberalization of trade. Although the Border Patrol interprets this smuggling method as a sign that law enforcement pressure has forced smugglers to take "desperate measures," the ability to move one hundred or more migrants across the border in a single truckload reflects a more developed transportation system than in the past. "You can't search every semi," one border agent points out. "You'd back up the whole border, and they [the smugglers] know that."[48] The higher stakes of the migrant-smuggling game have also sparked a technological race. Peter Skerry and Stephen Rockwell note that "as the Border Patrol pours more resources into night-vision scopes, weight sensors and giant X-ray machines for seeing into trucks, smuggling rings counter with their own state-of-the-art equipment paid for by increased [smuggling] fees."[49]

Thus, even as the small-time, freelance entrepreneurs who once dominated the smuggling business along the border are being weeded out by intensified enforcement, they are being replaced by better organized and more skilled groups. One INS intelligence report suggests that many smuggling operations once based in the United States have relocated to the Mexican side of the border to help insulate principal leaders from prosecution.[50] A multi-agency federal task force has estimated that ten to twelve family-based organizations dominate the trafficking of migrants across the U.S.-Mexico border.[51]

An unintended side effect of U.S. efforts to deter the maritime smuggling of Asian migrants has added to the challenge of dealing with organized migrant smuggling. The highly visible arrival of Chinese smuggling boats such as the *Golden Venture* in 1993 drew enormous media attention, helping to create an image that the United States was under siege and prompting a swift law enforcement crackdown. Smugglers responded by diverting much of the Asian migrant traffic to alternative routes, one of

47. Smugglers have reportedly created a network of fifty to sixty tunnels under the border city of El Paso; one exits next to City Hall and another under the Fort Bliss army base: Reuters, 21 October 1999.

48. Quoted in *New York Times*, 18 June 1999.

49. Peter Skerry and Stephen Rockwell, "The Cost of a Tighter Border: People-Smuggling Networks," *Los Angeles Times*, 3 May 1998.

50. U.S. General Accounting Office, *Illegal Immigration: Southwest Border Strategy Results Inconclusive; More Evaluation Needed* (Washington, D.C., December 1997), 42.

51. *Migration News*, June 1998.

which was through Mexico.[52] As Meissner noted, "We've stopped that illegal boat traffic, but there are still a lot of people coming from Asia, mainly through Central America and Mexico."[53] Indeed, a December 1995 federal study estimated that 100,000 illegal south Asian and Chinese immigrants travel through Central America and Mexico annually en route to the United States.[54] Such long-distance smuggling of non-Mexicans represents only a small percentage of illegal migration across the southwestern border, but it is certainly the most lucrative component of the business.

In response to tighter controls, the smuggling of migrants across the U.S.-Mexico border has become a more organized business, which has served to justify still tougher laws and tougher enforcement. The INS has had an antismuggling program since 1978, but smugglers were not aggressively targeted along the border until recent years.[55] For example, Operation Disruption, launched in May 1995 to detect "drop houses" in the San Diego area, produced the arrest of 120 smugglers and the uncovering of 117 drop houses.[56] The crackdown displaced much of the migrant smuggling eastward to the more rural Imperial Valley. The Border Patrol, in turn, responded with a nearly tenfold increase in the number of agents assigned to combat smuggling rings in that area.[57] Other federal agencies, such as the FBI, have also deployed new agents to the border to combat the increasingly organized traffic.[58]

The number of alien-smuggling cases prosecuted has skyrocketed. In San Diego, the busiest federal court in the country for migrant smuggling cases, prosecutions rose from 33 in 1993 to 233 in 1996, and have continued to increase.[59] Smugglers are now being sentenced to years rather than months in prison. Although the sharp growth in the number of arrests and in the severity of penalties has so far failed to curb smuggling, one federal prosecutor explains that the tougher policy is justified because it "sends a serious message" to smugglers and improves officer morale.[60]

Still, there appears to be no shortage of smugglers. As one official from the Border Patrol's anti-smuggling unit has noted, they "just get paid more

52. Author interview, National Security Council, Washington, D.C., 2 June 1997.
53. Quoted in *New York Times*, 30 May 1996.
54. Ibid.
55. Author interview with senior official in the Border Patrol's antismuggling unit, San Diego, Calif., 28 April 1997.
56. *Migration News*, 2 February 1996.
57. *Los Angeles Times*, 10 May 1998.
58. *Los Angeles Times*, 29 May 1996.
59. Department of Justice, *Annual Report of the Office of the United States Attorney, Southern District of California* (Washington, D.C., 1996).
60. Author interview, Office of the U.S. Attorney for the Southern District of California, San Diego, Calif., 28 April 1997.

for taking more risks."[61] Consequently, even though arresting more smugglers has provided an indicator for officials needing to show progress in controlling the border, it has not necessarily curbed smuggling. As one federal prosecutor has noted, there is a "Vietnam approach" in which progress against smugglers is measured by "body counts." To justify budgets, the "statistics monster must be fed."[62] At the same time, as the risks and penalties have risen, so has the smuggler's willingness to take more extreme measures to evade law enforcement. This partly explains the increase in the number of high-speed chases and accidents that occur when smugglers try to evade highway checkpoints near the border.

The heightened stakes have also exacerbated the corruption problem within the INS. In 1994 the *Dallas Morning News* reported that "no agency of the government is more vulnerable to corruption than the INS, where front-line workers, paid little more than the minimum wage, give out green cards and other coveted documents that are worth thousands on the black market."[63] The problem is obviously difficult to quantify, but current trends have only added to it. Michael Bromwich, the inspector general of the Department of Justice, noting the doubling of INS personnel along parts of the border since 1993, has warned, "Experience in other contexts indicates that massive law enforcement hirings may be accompanied by increased police corruption because of the greater susceptibility of new recruits to temptation or because corners may be cut in screening and training the new hires." Fraud and corruption allegations involving INS employees represent the single largest component of the caseload of the Office of Inspector General.[64] INS port inspectors are particularly vulnerable to corruption. They are in charge of the thinnest line of the deterrence effort, are hired locally (not routinely rotated to other posts along the border), are poorly paid, and have little supervision.[65]

Moreover, as border controls have increased, the incentive for smugglers to offer bribes or buy entry documents from those doing the controlling has also increased. And as smuggling groups have become more sophisticated, organized, and profitable (given the higher demand and cost

61. Author interview, U.S. Border Patrol, San Diego sector headquarters, San Diego, Calif., 8 April 1997.

62. Author interview, Office of the U.S. Attorney for the Southern District of California, San Diego, Calif., 1 April 1997.

63. *Dallas Morning News*, 11 September 1994.

64. Inspector General Bromwich, Senate Caucus on International Narcotics Control, *Threat and Effects of Corruption to U.S. Law Enforcement along the Mexican Broder*, 105th Cong., 1st sess., 14 May 1997, 5–6.

65. Author interview, Office of the U.S. Attorney for the Southern District of California, San Diego, Calif., 4 April 1997.

for their services and the heightened risks involved), the capacity and means to corrupt have also grown. Thus, bribing corrupt officials is like paying an entry fee—and the incentives both to pay and to collect the fee increase as traditional methods of entry become more difficult and risky.

THE NONESCALATION OF WORKPLACE ENFORCEMENT

The escalation of the U.S. effort to control illegal immigration has been highly selective. Noticeably downplayed in the rush to secure the border is the fact that some 40–50 percent of all illegal immigrants in the United States entered the country legally (perhaps as tourists or students) and then simply overstayed their visas. Roughly 150,000 people thus settle illegally in the country each year after entering legally. The neglect of visa overstays is itself a revealing indicator of how the symbolic importance of border control has overshadowed the stated policy goal of reducing the size of the illegal immigrant population. At the same time as Congress has pushed for an unprecedented increase in the size of the Border Patrol, little has been done to track down the holders of expired visas.

Similarly, while border enforcement has escalated, there has been a noticeable nonescalation in the enforcement of employer sanctions and workplace standards to deter the hiring of illegal immigrant labor. The U.S. Commission on Immigration Reform noted in a staff report that "by one measure, Operation Gatekeeper appears to have had little effect—the availability of workers in industries that are dependent on illegal alien labor."[66] In some industries, in fact, that reliance has actually increased as border controls have tightened. For example, the percentage of illegal workers in California's agricultural industry rose from less than 10 percent in 1990 to as high as 40 percent in 1997. At the same time, the Border Patrol was turning its attention away from California's agricultural fields and toward the border: while more than 2,000 agents cover the San Diego sector of the border, the number of agents north of Los Angeles has fallen from 65 to 22 in just a few years.[67]

The president's 1994 report on immigration stated, "Everyone agrees that the primary incentive for illegal immigration is employment. Workplace enforcement of labor standards and employer sanctions are the instruments for reducing that incentive."[68] Yet only about 2 percent of the

66. U.S. Commission on Immigration Reform, *Staff Report on Border Law Enforcement and Removal Initiatives in San Diego, California* (Washington, D.C., November 1995), 7.

67. *St. Louis Post-Dispatch*, 14 March 1999.

68. *Accepting the Immigration Challenge: The President's Report on Immigration* (Washington, D.C., 1994), 42.

INS budget is devoted to enforcing employer sanctions. When asked at a news conference why the lion's share of spending goes to border enforcement rather than focusing on the job magnet, Commissioner Meissner simply responded, "We have always argued that the centerpiece of effective enforcement must be the border, and that it must be backed up with employer enforcement."[69] In 1998, INS workplace investigations represented perhaps 3 percent of the nation's employers of unauthorized foreign workers, and most of those investigations did not result in penalties.[70]

There are only about 1,700 INS investigators assigned to cover the interior of the country, and less than a fifth of their time is devoted to worksite enforcement.[71] Thus, what John Shaw, the assistant INS commissioner for investigations, observed in 1993 seems even more true today: "There are 7.2 million employers out there. In their lifetime, they're never going to see an immigration officer unless they stand up and scream that they've got a factory full of illegal aliens."[72] For example, there were only about 6,000 INS investigations of employers for immigration violations in FY 1995, a drop from almost 15,000 in FY 1989. The number of fines against employers for hiring illegal immigrants fell from 2,000 in FY 1992 to 888 in FY 1997, and the total amount of the fines dropped from $17 million to $8 million.[73] Moreover, the INS generally settles cases for less than half the amount of the original fine.

In short, the employer sanctions established by IRCA in 1986 are notoriously weak and minimally enforced. Since employers are not required to verify the authenticity of documents, they risk little by hiring illegal immigrants—so long as they can present some form of documentation; the consequence is an expansive business in phony documents. According to Richard Rogers, head of the INS in Los Angeles, "You can buy a packet with a Social Security card and [green card] right now on the street for about $50 or $75, one sufficient for an employer to use as verification."[74]

The lack of attention to the workplace is a striking example of the enormous gap between expert opinion and policy practice. For example, the U.S. Commission on Immigration Reform concluded in a September 1994 report that "reducing the employment magnet is the linchpin of a comprehensive strategy to reduce illegal immigration."[75] The commission pro-

---

69. Doris Meissner press conference, 8 February 1996.

70. General Accounting Office, *Illegal Aliens: Significant Obstacles to Reducing Unauthorized Alien Employment Exist* (Washington, D.C., April 1999), 3.

71. *Washington Post,* 16 February 1997.

72. Quoted in Dick Kirschten, "Tempest-Tossed Task," *Government Executive,* October 1993.

73. *Migration News,* April 1996; *Migration News,* November 1998.

74. *San Diego Union-Tribune,* 2 November 1997.

75. *San Diego Union-Tribune,* 3 November 1997.

posed a national computer registry of the names and social security numbers of people authorized to work in the country, and pilot projects to use the registry in select states. Employers would be required to call a central number to check that the social security numbers of their workers were valid and issued to individuals authorized to work. Nevertheless, the sweeping immigration law passed by Congress in 1996 reaffirmed the policy focus on the border. The final legislation gutted the proposal for a mandatory verification system (opting instead for a limited "voluntary" pilot project) and rejected requirements for tamperproof birth certificates and driver's licenses.[76] Moreover, although an earlier version of the proposed legislation called for an increase in the number of Labor Department inspectors to enforce wage-and-hour laws and an increase in the penalties for employers who repeatedly hire illegal immigrant workers, these provisions were deleted in the final bill.[77] Thus, Congress, the most enthusiastic proponent of tough border controls, at the same time blocked efforts to enhance worksite enforcement. As the INS commissioner commented, "Being effective means making it hard for an illegal immigrant to get employment. Yet with this Congress, it's been an uphill battle to get resources for employer enforcement."[78]

The lack of meaningful workplace controls has helped to fuel more border controls. Inhibited from seriously targeting the workplace, politicians have had to rely on touting their support for border control to demonstrate their resolve in fighting illegal immigration. Moreover, lax workplace controls have assured that high levels of illegal immigration persist, creating more work for the Border Patrol, which in turn provides a rationale for more agents and resources.

The INS remains under an intense congressional spotlight—not because of its beefed-up border controls or its neglect of workplace controls but rather because it is not doing even more to police the border. Evaluations in congressional hearings tend to be narrowly focused on operational concerns—equipment and technology needs, agency coordination, hiring levels, and strategy implementation. The unquestioned assumption seems to be that the obstacle to effective deterrence is technical rather than any fundamental flaw in the control strategy itself. Being pushed hard by Congress, however, is what has made the INS grow so impressively in recent years. The adversarial relationship with Congress, in other words, is also symbiotic: the INS has been an easy target for politicians, but political attention has brought with it an unprecedented increase in enforcement

76. Ibid.
77. Associated Press, 25 September 1996.
78. Quoted in *New York Times Magazine,* 27 October 1996, 52.

resources.[79] Even as INS officials admit that the border-focused control strategy can have only a limited deterrent effect as long as workplace enforcement remains anemic (and complain about the reluctance of Congress to strengthen it), they have nevertheless welcomed the new political commitment to beefing up border controls.[80]

THE CONTRADICTIONS OF ECONOMIC INTEGRATION

It is an increasingly awkward problem for U.S. officials that even with the strong domestic political imperative to control the border more effectively, enforcement has become more difficult in the broader context of economic integration and market reform—which, in turn, further reinforces the push to improve border controls. According to the INS, "The Administration's goal is unambiguous: a border that deters illegal immigration, drug trafficking, and alien smuggling and facilitates legal immigration and commerce."[81] But this is much easier said than done. The president's 1994 report on immigration frankly acknowledged that "efforts to facilitate travel across the U.S.-Mexico border as part of the North American Free Trade Agreement may conflict with the need to establish closer controls on cross-border traffic to enforce immigration laws."[82]

The tension between facilitation and enforcement is played out on a daily basis at border ports of entry. At San Ysidro, the busiest land border crossing point in the world, "inspectors are frustrated that they must often choose between a thorough inspection which slows traffic or an expedited one that keeps traffic moving," according to the U.S. Commission for Immigration Reform.[83] Operation Gatekeeper has only added to the frustration, sparking a 40 percent rise in the use of fraudulent documents. The policy response has been a mixture of tougher penalties, a sharp increase in the number of port inspectors, and the testing of more technologically sophisticated traffic management procedures such as automated vehicle

79. Mark Reed, the INS district director in San Diego, explained that although the pressure and criticism from Congress may often be unfair and misplaced, in the end it helps his agency grow; it would be a far worse problem, reflected in past experience, if the INS were simply ignored. Author interview, San Diego, Calif., 1 May 1997.

80. Author interviews with INS officials in Washington, D.C., and San Diego, Calif., March and June 1997.

81. Immigration and Naturalization Service, *Building a Comprehensive Southwest Border Enforcement Strategy* (Washington, D.C., April 1996).

82. *Accepting the Immigration Challenge*, 42.

83. U.S. Commission on Immigration Reform, *Staff Report on Border Law Enforcement*, 14.

license-plate readers and a system that uses palm prints and fingerprints to verify the identity of individuals and reduce processing time.

Innovations in traffic management, however, have done little to tame the economic forces that have helped to maintain high levels of illegal immigration. Market integration and Mexico's own internal economic reforms are, at least in the short and medium term, adding to the incentives for Mexican workers to seek employment in the United States. As Robert Bach explained before he became a senior INS official (and a key proponent of border enforcement), "Increased market integration means the sending country's loss of control over its own labor supply. Although political tensions may increase . . . the demand for labor inside the United States will continue to dominate attempts to regulate the flow of immigrant workers."[84] In addition, the Mexican government's strategy to restructure the economy has been a labor-shedding process. Wayne Cornelius has pointed out that "even with a booming export sector," Mexico's neo-liberal economic development model "has much less capacity to create employment than the old import-substituting industrialization model that it replaced. Indeed, the new model's goals of efficiency and global competitiveness are inversely related to job creation."[85]

On the eve of the NAFTA vote, Attorney General Janet Reno argued that the passage of the trade accord would "help me protect our borders."[86] She even warned that if NAFTA failed, "effective immigration control [would] become impossible."[87] Without NAFTA, she said, illegal immigration was "only going to get worse. I don't have the numbers, but every bit of logic . . . would confirm it."[88] On the Mexican side, President Carlos Salinas promised that the passage of NAFTA would help Mexico export tomatoes rather than tomato pickers.

The aggressive political campaign to sell NAFTA, however, conveniently glossed over what Douglas Massey and Kristin Espinosa found obvious:

84. Robert L. Bach, "Hemispheric Migration in the 1990s," in *The United States and Latin America in the 1990s: Beyond the Cold War,* ed. Jonathan Hartlyn et al. (Chapel Hill: University of North Carolina Press, 1992), 274.

85. Wayne A. Cornelius, "The Immigration Issue in U.S.-Mexican Relations: A Structurally Determined Irritant" (paper prepared for Conference on Mexico and the United States in the Next Decade, Pacific Council on International Policy and Center for U.S.-Mexican Studies, University of California, San Diego, La Jolla, Calif., 11 May 1998), 15.

86. Janet Reno, "Consider NAFTA a Border Control Tool," *Los Angeles Times,* 22 October 1993.

87. Quoted in Wayne Cornelius and Philip Martin, "Perspective on NAFTA: Take the Long View of Immigration," *Los Angeles Times,* 2 November 1993.

88. Reuters Business Report, 1 November 1993.

The provisions of NAFTA . . . [will] help to bring about the social and economic transformations that generate migrants. The integration of the North American market will also create new links of transportation, telecommunication, and interpersonal acquaintance, connections that are necessary for the efficient movement of goods, information, and capital, but which also encourage and promote the movement of people—students, business executives, tourists, and, ultimately, undocumented workers.[89]

Although many immigration specialists predict that NAFTA (along with slowing birthrates in Mexico) will in the long term help to reduce cross-border labor flows, in the short and medium term the liberalization of trade actually helps to promote them.[90] This fact, of course, reinforces the already well-established cross-border social networks that provide a critical base and bridge for further immigration flows. In other words, since immigration is a cumulative process that builds on itself, even the hoped-for long-term reduction of illegal immigration is not at all assured.

NAFTA, it should be emphasized, is only one component of a much broader process of economic restructuring in Mexico that has helped stimulate illegal immigration.[91] Particularly important has been the liberalization of agriculture. Luis Téllez, the former undersecretary for planning in Mexico's Ministry of Agriculture and Hydraulic Resources, has estimated that as many as 15 million peasants will leave agriculture in the next decade or two.[92] Crossing the border in search of other work will no doubt be the most logical option for some.

Massive reductions in state assistance in rural areas are creating incentives to migrate.[93] Since the late 1980s the Mexican government has been cutting back electricity, fertilizer, water, and credit subsidies to peasant farmers; slashing price supports for many crops; and eliminating prohibitions on the sale of communal farm lands (about 70 percent of Mexico's cropland and half of its irrigated land). The government's income sub-

89. Douglas S. Massey and Kristin E. Espinosa, "What's Driving Mexico-U.S. Migration?—A Theoretical, Empirical, and Policy Analysis," *American Journal of Sociology* 102, no. 4 (1997): 991–92.

90. See Philip L. Martin, *Trade and Migration: NAFTA and Agriculture* (Washington, D.C.: Institute for International Economics, 1993).

91. See Monica L. Heppel and Luis R. Torres, *Migration in the Post-NAFTA Era: Policy Issues for the United States and Mexico* (Washington, D.C.: Center for Inter-Cultural Education and Development, Georgetown University, September 1995).

92. Cited in Philip L. Martin, "Mexican-U.S. Migration: Policies and Economic Impacts," *Challenge* (March 1995): 56–63.

93. See Santiago Levy and Sweder van Wijnbergen, *Transition Problems in Economic Reform: Agriculture in the Mexico-U.S. Free Trade Agreement,* Policy Research Working Papers (Washington, D.C.: World Bank, August 1992).

sidy program, initiated in late 1993 for producers of corn and other basic crops, has been a poor substitute for the kind of public investment (affordable credit, crop insurance, infrastructural improvements such as irrigation and drainage) needed to modernize Mexican agriculture and make small-scale farming truly viable.[94]

The collapse of the peso in December 1994, which plunged Mexico into the most severe recession in over half a century, added to the exit incentive. The devaluation of the peso further widened the U.S.-Mexico wage gap, increasing the incentive to earn dollar wages in the United States. In 1995 about 10 percent of jobs in the formal sector were lost. The private sector responded to the crisis by cutting jobs and lowering wages, and the subsequent economic recovery has not been followed by substantial gains in wages or employment. Meanwhile, a healthy U.S. economy has been a powerful magnet for low-skilled migrant labor.

Thus, even if left politely unmentioned in the official policy debate, illegal immigration has become an integral dimension of U.S.-Mexican economic interdependence. Mexico has become dependent on exporting part of its unemployment problem (which in turn has generated an estimated $6 billion in annual remittances from Mexican migrants),[95] and many U.S. employers have become dependent on the cheap labor provided by Mexican workers. And this mutual dependence, far from being reversed, has only been reinforced by the state-promoted process of economic restructuring and market liberalization. This is the less celebrated, clandestine side of U.S.-Mexico integration.

THE NEW IMAGE OF ORDER ON THE BORDER

Even in the face of these economic realities, U.S. officials have repeatedly praised the results of their border campaign to deter illegal immigration. In January 1996, in his State of the Union address, President Clinton highlighted his border enforcement record: "After years and years of neglect, this administration has taken on a strong stand to stiffen protection on our borders." Later that year the INS claimed that "the border is harder to cross now than at any time in history,"[96] and Doris Meissner boasted that the border strategy was "showing dramatic success."[97] Gus de la Viña, the

---

94. See Manuel Pastor Jr. and Carol Wise, "State Policy, Distribution, and Neoliberal Reform in Mexico," *Journal of Latin American Studies* 29, no. 2 (1997): 419–56.

95. A 1995 Mexican government survey found that some 600,000 Mexican households were receiving money from relatives in the United States: *San Diego Union-Tribune*, 31 October, 1999.

96. Immigration and Naturalization Service, *Operation Gatekeeper: Two Years of Progress* (Washington, D.C., October 1996).

chief of the Border Patrol, told a Senate committee in April 1999 that "we have achieved more in the past five years than had been accomplished in decades."[98]

Evaluations on the ground have been equally celebratory. Commenting on the results of Operation Gatekeeper, Johnny Williams, chief for the San Diego sector, boasted that it was "probably the single largest accomplishment in the Border Patrol's history."[99] Alan Bersin, who until mid-1998 was the attorney general's point person on the southwestern border, asserted that "for the first time in our history, we are moving decisively toward a border that functions effectively; one that is a lawful and orderly gateway; one that manages significantly better the problems of illegal immigration and smuggling; and one that promises and routinely delivers handsome dividends from an investment in regional integration."[100]

Most revealing about official statements, progress reports, and press releases, however, is what is not said: no claim is made or evidence presented that overall levels of illegal immigration have actually declined as a result of tighter border controls. Indeed, the INS has done little to formally evaluate the effectiveness of border deterrence. The GAO, in its 1997 assessment of the U.S. border control strategy, concluded that the INS lacked a formal process to determine the strategy's effectiveness systematically and comprehensively. Although the INS states that "the overarching goal of the strategy is to make it so difficult and so costly to enter this country illegally that fewer individuals even try," the GAO found that the INS and Justice Department had "no plans" for direct examination of the deterrent effect.[101]

There is no indication that large numbers of would-be border crossers are giving up in the face of tighter controls—and there is little reason to believe they will do so anytime soon.[102] Although "there is evidence the flows are shifting," one GAO official has explained, "what we are not see-

97. Testimony of INS Commissioner Doris Meissner, Senate Subcommittee on Immigration, Judiciary Committee, *Oversight of the Immigration and Naturalization Service*, 104th Cong., 2d sess., 2 October 1996.

98. Testimony of Gus de la Viña, chief of U.S. Border Patrol, Senate Subcommittee on Immigration, Judiciary Committee, *Border Patrol Operations and Staffing*, 106th Cong., 1st sess., 27 April 1999.

99. Quoted in *New York Times*, 28 August 1996.

100. Alan D. Bersin, "Reinventing the U.S.-Mexico Border," *San Diego Union-Tribune*, 25 August 1996.

101. General Accounting Office, *Illegal Immigration: Southwest Border Strategy Results Inconclusive* (Washington, D.C., December 1997).

102. See David Spener, "The Logic and Contradictions of Intensified Border Control in Texas," in *The Wall around the West: State Borders and Immigration Controls in North America and Europe*, ed. Peter Andreas and Timothy Snyder (Lantham, Md.: Rowman and Littlefield, 2000).

ing is people being discouraged from even trying."[103] Most migrants simply keep trying (sometimes being apprehended more than once in the same day) until they eventually make it across the line. Despite official threats of criminal prosecution for repeat crossings, limited detention space means that relatively few repeat offenders are ever prosecuted. As the Border Patrol's San Diego chief has candidly acknowledged, "When they run, we grab as many as we can. We take them back to the border and they try again. Eventually, most of them get through."[104]

Even in the face of the massive border buildup, the number of unauthorized immigrants in the country has grown by an estimated 275,000 per year. Approximately 6 million illegal immigrants now live in the United States.[105] Judged purely on its instrumental deterrent effect, then, the current border control strategy's political popularity seems puzzling. But a failing policy can still succeed politically. In this case, the border *appears* more orderly because much greater control has in fact been imposed at the urban crossing points most visible to the media and the public. As the Border Patrol puts it, "The daily chaos which reigned along the San Diego border has, at long last, been replaced by scenes of control and order."[106] Gone are the images of the "Banzai runs" that helped reelect Pete Wilson and fanned the flames of the anti-immigrant backlash in California. In just a few years, a powerful image of control has been successfully projected through a high-profile deployment of enforcement resources and personnel along what were once highly contested sections of the border. In truth, however, unauthorized crossings are much less visible because they are more dispersed, more remote, and more hidden. "Sealing the border is an impossible mission," one researcher from the University of Texas at El Paso has noted. "Chief Reyes [the El Paso sector Border Patrol chief who launched operation Hold-the-Line] has compromised by making the problem invisible. In that sense, he's been successful."[107]

The new image of order is powerfully captured by two of the Border Patrol's public relations videos. The first, titled *Border under Siege,* was made in 1992. The narrator describes the border as "less a boundary than a backdoor." The second video, less dramatically titled *Challenge on the Border,* was produced in 1996 and projects an entirely different message. The first video depicts the border as being overwhelmed by clandestine crossers; the second video is largely self-congratulatory, applauding the

103. Quoted in *San Antonio Express News,* 20 May 1999.
104. Quoted in *San Diego Union-Tribune,* 14 January 1996.
105. *Washington Post,* 15 March 1999; *Washington Post,* 17 February 2000.
106. Quoted in *Christian Science Monitor,* 4 October 1999.
107. Quoted in *Dallas Morning News,* 22 October 1995.

Border Patrol for finally securing the border so that it "is no longer an open backdoor."

The border, of course, actually has many back doors. Closing some of them has moved, not removed, the clandestine population flow. In the case of Gatekeeper, "the game is to try and focus as much attention as possible on one small piece of real estate," explains T. J. Bonner, the president of the National Border Patrol Council. "You then hope everyone ignores the fact that we're being totally overrun in the rest of the sector." The truth, Bonner says, is that "it's bursting out all over—Arizona, New Mexico, parts of Texas. I don't see how that translates into success."[108]

From the political perspective of those charged with the task of border management, however, the way the media and the public *see* the border is more critical than actual deterrence. Pushing much of the migration flow out of sight has also helped push it out of the public's mind, and media coverage reinforces the new look of order. "Canyons once crowded with illegal crossers," glowed the *Los Angeles Times* in 1998, "are empty of all but sturdy new fences and the border agents who have poured into the region by the hundreds. Migrants no longer sprint en masse through the San Ysidro port of entry onto freeways."[109]

Ironically, some of the most perverse and counterproductive effects of the border deterrence effort have actually contributed to making the border appear more orderly and secure. For example, the tightening of controls has encouraged illegal migrants to cross the border fewer times but, once across, to stay longer in the United States. The traditional pattern was that most Mexicans who came illegally did not stay but went back and forth in what amounted to cross-border commuting. The increased risk and cost of crossing the border, however, also increased the incentive for many illegal immigrants to extend their stay or perhaps even to settle down permanently. In short, the more difficult and costly the commute, the greater the incentive to relocate closer to the workplace—a trend confirmed in a number of empirical studies.[110]

If the goal is to reduce the size of the unauthorized immigrant population in the United States, this outcome is an indicator of not only a failed but a counterproductive policy. Yet by contributing to the policy goal of reducing the number of illegal border crossings, it has enhanced the appearance of order. When a 1997 Urban Institute study found that illegal

108. Quoted in *Los Angeles Times*, 6 July 1996.
109. *Los Angeles Times*, 28 June 1998.
110. See, for example, Frank Bean et al., *Illegal Mexican Migration and the United States-Mexican Border: The Effects of Operation "Hold the Line" on El Paso/Juarez* (Austin: Population Research Center, University of Texas, and U.S. Commission on Immigration Reform, 1994).

immigrants in California were remaining in the state for longer periods of time due to tighter border controls, the INS responded, "This is another sign that our efforts to control the border are working."[111]

The powerful image effect and symbolic appeal of enhanced border policing has so far not only overshadowed its failings and flaws but made it rewarding for its architects. For the INS, the border campaign has brought with it unprecedented organizational growth and political commitment to a long-neglected and much-maligned agency. For elected leaders, it has won votes, provided a politically costless method of signaling that they are "tough" on illegal immigration, and helped inoculate Democrats against Republican attacks that they are "soft on illegals." As stated in the 1996 Democratic Party platform: "For years before Bill Clinton became President, Washington talked tough but failed to act. In 1992, our borders might as well not have existed. The border was under-patrolled, and what patrols there were, were under-equipped." The platform credited Clinton for reversing this history of neglect: "President Clinton is making our border a place where the law is respected and drugs and illegal immigrants are turned away."[112]

In the 1996 presidential race, beefed-up border controls provided Clinton with a powerful political shield against Republican attack, especially in the politically vital state of California. In June a Republican National Committee television ad highlighted a border entry point marked "Mexico" and then showed what were presumably illegal immigrants running across the line in the glare of spotlights; "Under President Clinton," it declared, "spending on illegals has gone up, while wages for the typical worker have gone down." The Democratic National Committee quickly counterattacked with an ad showing what were presumably illegal immigrants being handcuffed. The ad emphasized that Clinton had significantly beefed up the size of the Border Patrol and displayed scenes from the Republican ad with the word WRONG stamped in red letters.[113] Both of these television campaign advertisements were run most often in California, where anxiety over illegal immigration has been highest. Clinton handily won the war of images: in the November election he not only took California as a whole but prevailed even in the conservative stronghold of Orange County—the birthplace of Proposition 187. In other words, the images of a chaotic border that were so masterfully exploited by Governor Wilson in 1994 were unavailable for Bob Dole in 1996. The administration's border control offensive had successfully erased them.

111. *New York Times*, 12 October 1997.

112. The Democratic Party's 1996 National Platform, quoted in Nevins, "Illegal Aliens," 4–5.

113. Dick Kirschten, "Crossing the Line," *National Journal* 3 (August 1996): 1422–27.

In his autobiographical account of his experience as labor secretary during the first Clinton administration, Robert Reich recalls that one week before the November 1996 elections, Mark Penn, a chief pollster for the campaign, gave a presentation at the White House in which he explained how Clinton had gone from trailing the Republican candidate by ten points to leading by twenty points: he did so "by coopting the Republicans on all their issues—getting tough on welfare, tough on crime, balancing the budget, and cracking down on illegal immigration."[114] Penn then showed video tapes of campaign advertisements that emphasized these themes. Given this account, it should not be surprising that Clinton has been accused of taking credit for Republican initiatives. As Representative Duncan Hunter (R-Calif.), has complained, "I build fences and put Border Patrol in the budget and they [Clinton officials] do all the press conferences."[115]

High-profile immigration control initiatives such as Operations Hold-the-Line and Gatekeeper have transformed the landscape of the southwestern border. This has meant not necessarily a reduction in illegal immigration but rather a reinvention of the image of the border. The border control offensive has not only been the latest move in an endless game of cat and mouse but reflected a fundamental change in the rules of the game itself: the most visible form of clandestine entry—groups of illegal migrants openly crossing the border near urban areas—is no longer politically tolerable. Thus, for the border crossers, evading apprehension has become a longer and more complex game requiring greater patience and stealth. With persistence, they eventually make it across the line, but in a less visible (and thus less politically embarrassing) manner than before. In other words, the old game between border enforcers and clandestine border crossers persists, but the game strategy of the enforcers has changed to maximize the appearance of control. Projecting a "winning image," it seems, has so far provided a politically viable alternative to actually winning the game.

That image has come at an enormous cost: more intensive border policing has brought with it more (and more organized) professional smuggling, greater corruption, and many border deaths.[116] But at least for now, these negative consequences have been obscured by the powerful political and symbolic appeal of a border that appears more orderly and secure. At the same time, however, it should be emphasized that the deterrence ef-

114. Robert B. Reich, *Locked in the Cabinet* (New York: Knopf, 1997), 329.

115. Quoted in *Los Angeles Times*, 28 June 1998.

116. A 1997 report by researchers at the University of Houston found that over the previous four years, 1,185 people had drowned, died of exposure or dehydration, or been hit by automobiles while trying to cross the border between official ports of entry: *New York Times*, 24 August 1997.

fort has created the conditions for its own expansion, since the shifts in the methods and location of illegal border crossings have in turn placed new demands on the law enforcement system to adjust and keep up. Indeed, as envisioned by the Border Patrol, current enforcement levels are just the beginning of a long-term buildup.[117] Operation Gatekeeper, the San Diego sector chief has explained, was a "demonstration project." Once it was shown that the most contested piece of the border could be significantly controlled with an infusion of resources, it was assumed that a similar show of force would work elsewhere. As one agent put it, "We are taking back the border, piece by piece."[118]

117. *Border Patrol Strategic Plan 1994 and Beyond,* 12.

118. Author interview, U.S. Border Patrol San Diego sector headquarters, San Diego, Calif., 4 March 1997.

Part III

Extensions and Conclusions

CHAPTER SIX

Policing the External Borders of the New Europe

For comparative insight, it is useful to extend the analysis to other borders in other regions where rich and poor countries intersect. At first glance, two of the European Union's key external borders—between Germany and Poland, and between Spain and Morocco—seem strikingly similar to the U.S.-Mexico case: there is the same rapid escalation of state efforts to police illegal cross-border flows, even while facilitating and encouraging more cross-border economic exchange. A closer examination, however, reveals significant variation in the methods, intensity, and focus of policing; the messages and images communicated by such policing; and the audiences to whom these are communicated. The differences reflect both distinct historical legacies and diverse regional, political, and institutional contexts.

THE SHIFTING BORDERS OF THE NEW EUROPE

The borders of Western Europe have been radically transformed since the end of the Cold War and the collapse of the Soviet Union. The lifting of the Iron Curtain shattered the traditional military rationale for fortified borders but at the same time reinforced calls to create a "Fortress Europe" against the perceived threats of clandestine immigration, drug trafficking, and other unwanted cross-border activities. Thus, the celebratory mood that accompanied the opening of the East was quickly soured by rising anxiety over a potential mass influx of "undesirables." Ironically, the authoritarian controls of the eastern bloc, which had placed severe checks on cross-border movement, were nostalgically missed. In short, concerns over law evasions rather than military invasions soon emerged as the new post–Cold War security priority in Western Europe. As Monica den Boer observed, "In a new Europe where military activities are in the process of being dismantled, the police forces are moving into the confines of international security protection."[1]

Anxiety over perceived new threats was exacerbated by plans to dismantle internal border controls during European integration. The dream of a border-free European Union, envisioned by the Single European Act of 1986, was paralleled by nightmare images of a potential border-free Europe open to illegal activity. Since it was widely assumed that the internal borders of Western Europe provided a filter against unlawful border crossings, it was also assumed that erasing those borders would encourage such crossings. But the original assumption was questionable, given how permeable the internal borders had already become before 1992. In the case of illegal drugs, for example, "contrary to what the general public often believes," noted Georges Estievenart of the European Commission's Drugs Monitoring Centre, "the physical internal frontiers of the Community have long ceased to be the strategic spot where most drug hauls and arrests of traffickers take place." In 1991, for example, 72.9 percent of hashish confiscations, 88.8 percent of marijuana, 53.5 percent of heroin, and 86.1 percent of cocaine occurred at the *external* borders of the European Community.[2]

But even though the filter function of the internal borders was more myth than reality, part of what worried European officials was that the formal opening of these borders would make them *appear* more open to illegal activity, expose the myth of control, undermine the credibility of state authority, and fuel public apprehension and fear. Entrepreneurial state officials—reinforced by media coverage—played up these concerns and lobbied for compensatory measures to cope with the "internal security gap" that would presumably arise with the lifting of internal border checks.[3] European economic integration and the opening of the internal borders have provided the primary rationale for heightened cross-border

1. Monica den Boer, "Moving between Bogus and Bona Fide: The Policing of Inclusion and Exclusion in Europe," in *Migration and European Integration: The Dynamics of Inclusion and Exclusion,* ed. Robert Miles and Dietrich Thränhardt (London: Pinter, 1995), 107.

2. Georges Estievenart, "The European Community and the Global Drug Phenomenon: Current Situation and Outlook," in *Policies and Strategies to Combat Drugs in Europe,* ed. Georges Estievenart et al. (Norwell, Mass.: Kluwer Academic Publishers, 1995), 58–59.

3. As noted in Malcolm Anderson, et al., *Policing the European Union* (New York: Oxford University Press, 1996), 61, the elimination of internal border controls "has certainly been exploited by police and security services in order to gain a broader mandate, more resources and better equipment."

police collaboration and tighter external border controls. EU members have harmonized parts of their criminal justice systems, and policing cooperation has become much more institutionalized. The aim of European policing collaboration has been to create a "security surplus" instead of a "security deficit." This has meant establishing a "'cordon sanitaire' to keep out drug traffickers, terrorists and other criminals, refugees together with unwanted immigrants. Greatly increased cooperation between police and judicial authorities, shared intelligence and stricter internal controls would offset the consequences of permitting these undesirables—if they have breached the perimeter fence—to circulate freely around Europe."[4]

European police cooperation has primarily taken the form of intergovernmental arrangements, the most important of which were the Schengen Accords: the initial agreement of 1985 and the later implementation agreement of 1990. The EU signatories to Schengen agreed to abolish internal border checks while also harmonizing and tightening external border checks.[5] These included the development of a common—and much more restrictive—visa policy and asylum-processing procedure and the creation of a shared computer system for information exchange (the "Schengen Information System").[6] Thus, what once were treated exclusively as national borders and national controls have become part of a new European space of free movement protected by a hardened outer wall. Two of the most important and contested sections of this new EU wall are the eastern border of Germany and the southern border of Spain.

THE ESCALATION OF POLICING ACROSS THE GERMAN-POLISH BORDER

The Oder and Neisse Rivers, which form the boundary between Germany and Poland, have been called "the Río Grande of Europe." Heinrich

4. House of Lords Select Committee on the European Communities, quoted in Eugene McLaughlin, "The Democratic Deficit: European Union and the Accountability of the British Police," *British Journal of Criminology* 32, no. 4 (1992): 481.

5. The Schengen Accords were formally superseded by the Treaty of Amsterdam, signed 2 October 1997 and effective 1 May 1999. The Schengen institutional structures and practices are now incorporated into the formal framework of the EU and the Treaty of the European Union. This shifts responsibility for immigration policies from individual governments to the European Commission.

6. "The loss of some sovereignty is apparently regarded by most, if not all, Schengen states as a price worth paying to produce an enhanced capability to combat crime, limit clandestine immigration, and enable all internal border controls to be removed": John Benyon, "Policing the European Union: The Changing Basis of Cooperation on Law Enforcement," *International Affairs* 70, no. 3 (1994): 507.

Vogel, of the Cologne-based Institute for East European and International Studies, notes the "strong economic and social parallels" between the U.S.-Mexico and German-Polish relationships.[7] In few other geographic locations do poor and rich countries so intimately meet. Most important for this discussion, the German-Polish border, like the U.S.-Mexico border, has been turned into both a police barrier and an increasingly important economic bridge.

Even as the Berlin Wall and the militarized border between West and East Germany disappeared, the eastern border of a unified Germany became the site of intensive policing. According to German Interior Minister Manfred Kanther, "There is no higher police density along any other border in Europe."[8] The primary targets are smuggled illegal migrants, drugs, untaxed cigarettes, and stolen cars.

The flow of illegal immigrants across Germany's eastern border rose sharply after the collapse of the eastern bloc and German unification. In an October 1991 speech before the ministers responsible for immigration, Home Minister Wolfgang Schauble estimated that there were half a million illegal immigrants in Germany and that the number of illegal entries in 1991 alone was 200,000. Most of these, he claimed, had entered the country across the eastern border.[9] At the same time, the end of the Cold War opened up new source countries and trafficking routes to supply German and other West European drug consumers. For example, Poland has become one of the world's leading producers of illicit amphetamines—supplying an estimated 20–50 percent of the West European market[10]—and an important transshipment point for cocaine, cannabis, and heroin destined for Germany and the rest of the EU. Moreover, the smuggling of untaxed cigarettes across Germany's eastern border (estimated at 8–10 billion cigarettes a year) costs the German government $700 million annually in lost tax revenue.

Thus, perhaps not surprisingly, some German law enforcement officials now miss the policing benefits previously provided by the Iron Curtain: "The wall that the GDR [German Democratic Republic] erected to 'protect' socialism not only prevented GDR citizens from leaving their country, but also had the function of a bulwark for the internal security of the Federal Republic of Germany, since threats to the internal security of the

7. Quoted in *Los Angeles Times,* 1 September 1991.

8. Quoted in *Hamburg DPA,* 29 March 1996 (translated by Foreign Broadcast Information Service, 16 April 1996).

9. Cited in Bernhard Santel, "Loss of Control: The Build-up of a European Migration and Asylum Regime," in Miles and Thränhardt, *Migration and European Integration,* 78.

10. Geopolitical Drug Watch, *World Geopolitics of Drugs, 1995–1996 Annual Report* (Paris: Geopolitical Drug Watch, 1997).

FRG, posed by people coming over the border without passport checks, could be ruled out."[11]

Among the clandestine flows targeted by German border controls, illegal immigration has clearly been the leading enforcement concern. Crumbling authoritarian systems, political instability, the shocks of market-based economic restructuring, improved transportation and communications links to the West, and the lure of better-paying jobs have provided powerful incentives for many to migrate illegally to Germany (or to other European Union countries via Germany). The migrants come not only from East European countries such as Romania, Albania, and the former Yugoslavia but also from more distant lands such as Bangladesh and Afghanistan. Clandestine efforts to cross the German border are also partly a predictable consequence of the tightening of Germany's asylum laws in May 1993. The German (and broader EU) strategy for reducing asylum applications was to define Poland and other immediate eastern neighbors as "safe" countries, meaning that asylum-seekers who cross through these countries en route to Germany can be immediately deported. As one Berlin-based immigration specialist has noted, "The joke is that the only way that anyone can claim asylum in Germany nowadays is by parachuting in."[12] No longer able to apply for political asylum at border crossings, many foreigners have instead opted to enter Germany illegally.

Germany has dramatically expanded its policing apparatus not only at land borders but at air and seaports as well. For example, enforcement personnel at the Frankfurt airport have more than tripled since the early 1990s. The Bundesgrenzschutz (BGS), Germany's federal border police force, has been restructured to carry out its new and expanding duties: its budget more than doubled between 1990 and 1995, and its size tripled between 1993 and 1998.[13] Another sign of its rapid growth is that its operational headquarters in Koblenz expanded from one building in 1992 to four buildings in 1996.[14] A 1994 law extended the intensive search jurisdiction of the BGS in the border zone from two kilometers to thirty kilometers inland from the borderline, and it has been given the responsibility of policing airports and train stations as well. But its single most intensively targeted area is the German-Polish border: from about 400 bor-

11. Fritz Ulrich Maier, quoted in Albrecht Funk, "Control Myths: The Eastern Border of the Federal Republic of Germany before and after 1989" (paper prepared for the Police and Immigration toward a Europe of Internal Security, ECPR workshop, Madrid, Spain, 18–22 April 1994), 1.

12. Andreas Muster, quoted in *Houston Chronicle,* 7 December 1998.

13. Deutsche Presse-Agentur, 29 August 1995; *Sunday Telegraph* (London), 6 December 1998.

14. Author interview, BGS headquarters, Koblenz, Germany, 3 July 1996.

der guards there in 1990–91, the number had increased to some 3,300 by mid-1996.[15]

Created as a paramilitary force after World War II to protect West Germany's eastern border, the BGS in the post–Cold War era has been fighting border crimes rather than deterring Communists. As Manfred Kanther has explained, "Today, the BGS need no longer make sure at the border that the communists do not climb over the barbed wire but must pay attention to stolen cars, smuggled weapons and drugs, and to gangs of alien smugglers."[16] Most of the guards along Germany's eastern border now are former GDR guards.[17] It is perhaps ironic that whereas their original mission was to keep people in eastern Germany, their post–Cold War mission is to keep them out—and, of course, they can no longer use the land mines and "shoot to kill" methods of the past.

As on the U.S.-Mexico border, the tightening of German border controls has failed to deter illegal crossings significantly: the BGS has estimated that only one in five clandestine entrants are apprehended.[18] Tighter controls have, however, forced more illegal immigrants to hire professional smugglers, who charge about $900 just for the border crossing (and thousands more for the complete trip from countries such as Romania and Albania).[19] The migrant-smuggling business has boomed. "Each year, we are finding [that] more and more illegal entrants have been getting help from professional smugglers," according to BGS officers. "We create the business for the smuggler. We remove 100 aliens, and the smugglers bring 100 back in."[20]

In 1997 more than 500 smugglers were arrested.[21] Increased arrests, however, have so far failed to curb smuggling. Indeed, an 18 May 1998 report by Germany's intelligence service warned of a potentially "violent and uncontrollable rise" in human smuggling.[22] The interaction between the BGS and the smugglers is "an elaborate game," explains one officer, "and they're getting better at it every day."[23] The BGS claims that small-scale migrant smuggling is being replaced by more organized international criminal groups engaged in a variety of smuggling activities.[24] And this, paralleling the U.S.-Mexico border experience, has provided a ratio-

15. Author interview with BGS officials, Frankfurt-Oder, Germany, 24 June 1996.

16. Quoted in *Berlin Die Welt,* 21 November 1995 (translated by Foreign Broadcast Information Service, 21 December 1995).

17. Author interview with BGS officials, Frankfurt-Oder, Germany, 24 June 1996.

18. *Migration News,* June 1998.

19. Reuters, 9 November 1998.

20. Author interview with BGS officials, Eisenhüttenstadt, Germany, 24 June 1996.

21. *Wall Street Journal,* 4 May 1998.

22. *Migration News,* June 1998.

23. Quoted in *Wall Street Journal,* 4 May 1998.

24. Grenzschutzdirektion, *Report on Illegal Entry* (Koblenz, Germany, n.d.).

nale for increasingly defining illegal immigration as an organized-crime problem.

As in the United States, German law enforcement officials also face the growing challenge of trying to deter illegal border crossings while at the same time encouraging the rising volume of legal crossings. For example, 147 million people legally crossed the German-Polish border in 1994—a 250 percent increase over 1991—and the number of vehicles rose from approximately 7.2 million in 1990 to 60 million in 1994.[25] Even though the number of customs agents along the German-Polish border has increased significantly (in the German border state of Brandenburg it roughly doubled between 1991 and 1996),[26] the sharp growth of cross-border traffic has strained the capacity of law enforcement to separate legal from illegal crossings.

New ports of entry have been opened to encourage and facilitate cross-border exchange. For example, at the German border crossing of Kristrin, a port of entry for passenger vehicles was established for the first time in 1992, plus a new facility to handle commercial traffic. On weekends there are traffic jams up to 7.5 kilometers long, made up mostly of Germans on shopping excursions to Poland. As the number of legal crossings has skyrocketed, so too has the number of arrests for attempted illegal entry.[27] At the Frankfurt-Oder port of entry for commercial trucks, the number of vehicles crossing the border in both directions increased from 197,000 in 1989 to 547,000 in 1995 and had reached a million by 1998. Since only a small percentage of the trucks are inspected, an increasingly popular method of migrant smuggling has been to hide migrants within commercial cargo being trucked across the border[28] (a method that has also become more common along the U.S.-Mexico border). German officials have responded by using carbon dioxide sensors to determine whether truck loads are hiding human cargo.

Drug-smuggling routes into Germany have also followed the patterns of legitimate commerce.[29] Much of the heroin shipped through Poland to Germany and the rest of the EU is organized by Turkish trafficking networks that use commercial trucking to camouflage their business; Turkish transport companies run the largest fleet of cargo trucks in Europe.[30]

25. *Wall Street Journal,* 10 May 1995.

26. Author interview with German customs officials, Frankfurt-Oder, 25 June 1996.

27. Author interview with port inspectors, Kristrin border crossing, Germany, 24 June 1996.

28. Grenzschutzdirektion, *Report on Illegal Entry.*

29. Testimony of Hans-Ludwig Zachert, president of the German Federal Criminal Police, Senate Committee on Governmental Affairs, *Organized Crime in the Former Soviet Union,* 103d Cong., 2d sess., 25 May 1994.

30. International Criminal Police Organization (INTERPOL), *The European Heroin Scene, 1995–1996* (Lyons, France, 1997).

But although policing trends along the German-Polish border clearly overlap in many ways with those on the U.S.-Mexico border, there are profound differences between the two cases. For one thing, the German law enforcement strategy is less visible than the U.S. strategy, yet it is also in many ways both more intensive and more extensive. Although the deployment of German law enforcement resources and personnel to the eastern border has paralleled the expansion of U.S. policing along the southwestern border, the stadium lights, steel fencing, and automated cameras and sensors favored in the United States are noticeably missing. As one senior German law enforcement official has explained, "Some of the border control methods used by the United States are inconceivable here."[31] The legacy of the country's authoritarian past and recent memories of the Berlin Wall have inhibited the use of the more high-profile policing and surveillance methods.

Whereas U.S. officials are quick to emphasize the high-tech aspects of their border strategy, German officials have self-consciously tried to avoid creating the image of building an "electronic Iron Curtain." Although there are mobile night-vision cameras mounted on vans (costing $200,000 apiece), there are no stationary surveillance cameras on fixed posts along Germany's eastern border.[32] Nor has the German military played the same support role as the U.S. military. Indeed, when German military personnel were temporarily sent to the border in the early 1990s for the initial operation of some of the surveillance equipment, they wore police uniforms.[33] "Our different history gives us some different attitudes than the Americans," explains one border official. "We do not want fences and walls."[34] Consequently, compared with that of the United States, the German border strategy is less high-tech and more labor intensive.

Historical sensitivities also mean that German officials have been careful to explain and justify the tightening of the eastern border not simply as a German initiative but as part of a broader European policy on common external border controls, as outlined in the Schengen Accords. Embedding the tightened German controls in a larger European framework dampens the appearance of a unilateral reassertion of German territorial sovereignty. In immigration matters in general, such as asylum policy, German leaders have promoted their increasingly restrictive policies as measures necessary to conform to wider European standards. External border enforcement in particular has been legitimized as performing a European

31. Author interview with federal investigative police, Wiesbaden, Germany, 1 July 1996.
32. *Wall Street Journal*, 4 May 1998.
33. Statewatch, *Report on the Border Tour of the New Walls of Europe (29 October–3 November 1993)* (London: Statewatch, February 1994).
34. Quoted in *Houston Chronicle*, 7 December 1998.

function rather than as simply serving German national interest. In the United States, by contrast, it is precisely the image of defending and re-asserting national sovereignty that officials have tried to convey.

The multilateral framework provided by Schengen has enabled German policymakers to pacify conflicting audiences. Political elites have used Schengen to keep the extreme right at bay by showing that they are being tough on illegal immigration and, at the same time, to pacify advocates of migrant rights on the left by throwing up their hands and saying they have little choice but to be tough because of their obligations to Schengen. Schengen also helps to tame foreign anxieties about a resurgent Germany. The Europeanization of the German border and of German border controls through Schengen has helped to inhibit external fears of an aggressive unilateral reassertion of German power. Binding national policing to regional agreements has made German power less visible and controversial—even as it has arguably become more widespread and influential.[35]

Germany's co-optive relationship with Poland on immigration control further illustrates how the exercise of German power differs from that of the United States in relation to Mexico. Whereas Mexicans wishing to en-ter the United States are required to obtain a visa, Polish citizens can now enter Germany visa-free. This means that German efforts to deter clandes-tine entry along the border focus on non-Polish illegal immigrants who use Poland as an entry point to Germany and the rest of the EU. Therefore, even though many Poles illegally work in Germany and other EU coun-tries, the lack of a visa requirement puts their point of confrontation with law enforcement at the workplace rather than at the border. This fact has the political advantage of both diminishing the role of the border as a source of conflict between Germany and Poland and enhancing the image of the border as both open and secure.

It should also be emphasized that the German-Polish border is far more ambiguous than the U.S.-Mexico border because Poland is expected to join the EU soon. The carrot of future entry into the EU has helped to as-sure Poland's cooperation in stemming the smuggling of migrants through its territory. As agreed in a treaty that took effect in March 1993, Poland now takes back those who attempt to enter Germany illegally, while Ger-many provides funds as compensation. Germany has also helped Poland beef up the policing of its own 774-mile eastern border; for example, Ger-many allocated $80 million to Poland in 1994 for border-control pur-poses. Thus, the traditional role of Polish border guards has been entirely reversed: they now use resources from their former Western foes to guard

---

35. See Peter J. Katzenstein, *West Germany's Internal Security Policy*, Western Societies Paper no. 28 (Ithaca: Cornell University, 1990), 43.

against threats from former Eastern allies. Jeeps and weapons from the Soviet era have been replaced by British Land-Rovers and Austrian guns. "It was hard to expect that history would turn this way," observed one Polish border officer. "But we have always been part of Europe."[36]

The German (and broader EU) control strategy has been to use Poland and other central European countries as a buffer zone. Germany has co-opted Poland by means of preferential treatment: waiving the visa requirement for Poles seeking entry into the EU, providing temporary legal employment for many Poles in Germany, and backing Poland's application for future EU membership—which will further extend the EU's eastern border.

Changes in Polish immigration policy have consequently been driven by EU and especially German policy priorities. Tightened immigration controls mean that illegal migrants traveling to Germany through Poland must now get past both Polish and German border police. In 1996 it was reported that ten new watchtowers were being built and helicopters would start to patrol Poland's borders—including the Polish-Lithuanian border, which has become a hot spot for the smuggling of people and goods.[37] The Polish border guards are assisted by soldiers from the Wisla Military Units of the Ministry of Internal Affairs and Administration.[38] In 1999 the Polish government spent $8.5 million to reinforce its border force—five times more than in 1998—and claims that its 14,000 border guards still need to be increased by about 30 percent. Poland has also spent $24 million of EU funds to tighten controls on its eastern border and expects to build eighteen new posts there by the year 2002.[39]

Poland has been placed in the "unenviable position of acting as western Europe's eastern filter for migrants," researchers have concluded. "Embedded in multilateral arrangements, bilateral deals have created a new, more restrictive migration regime in which Poland acts as Germany's most important eastern gatekeeper."[40] Yet Poland seems to have accepted its role as a buffer state, recognizing that future EU membership is contingent on tougher immigration controls. As Maciej Kuczynski, the deputy director of the Department of Migration and Refugee Affairs, has explained it, "If we want to integrate into the European Union, we have to show our goodwill in fighting illegal immigration. If there is any risk that Poland will be a hole in the European border, we will not get in. We are very

36. Associated Press, 2 March 1999.
37. *Trafficking in Migrants Quarterly Bulletin,* June 1996.
38. *Zycie Warszawy* (Warsaw), 10 April 1999.
39. Associated Press, 2 March 1999.
40. Wlodek Aniol et al., "Returning to Europe: Central Europe between Internationalization and Institutionalization," in *Tamed Power: Germany in the New Europe,* ed. Peter J. Katzenstein (Ithaca: Cornell University Press, 1997), 218.

aware of that."[41] The political imperative to tighten controls, however, is at odds with Poland's need to keep its borders open to the traders and consumers—both legal and illegal—that have provided a boost to the local economy. In 1996, for example, 82 million foreigners entered Poland legally, primarily for shopping, and "We are being very careful not to take measures that kill the border commerce," Kuczynski has said.[42] In 1999 the Polish Ministry of Labor estimated that up to 200,000 illegal immigrants were living in Poland.[43]

It is also important to emphasize that the German immigration control strategy not only extends outward by using neighbors as a buffer but also extends inward. Germany has extensive internal controls, including the kind of workplace regulations that would meet stiff resistance from U.S. employers long accustomed to minimal state intervention. German penalties for hiring illegal foreign labor are both more common and more severe; for example, employer fines include the profits earned by employing illegal workers. In general, Germany's highly regulated and centralized labor market facilitates workplace monitoring. The Labor Office has more than 2,000 people to control the workplace.[44] The Labor Office has reported that it detected 406,000 cases of illegal employment in 1998 (mostly in construction) and imposed fines of DM225 million.[45] Moreover, the German Customs Service, which traditionally focused on collecting import and export duty, was restructured in 1994 to include an office to investigate illegal employment and check social security cards.[46] Thus, even as some functions of the service have been scaled back because of European integration, it has taken on new tasks.

German authorities rely on a mandatory resident registration system and national identification cards. Anyone applying for work must show the ID card to the employer, who in turn is required to report the number to the local labor office. Although identification cards are widely viewed in the United States as an unacceptable threat to civil liberties, they are noncontroversial in Germany and are needed not only for employment but also for accessing many public services, licensing, and even opening a bank account.[47] The emphasis on documents allows the government to draft

41. Quoted in *Los Angeles Times,* 27 December 1997.

42. Ibid.

43. *Rzeczpospolita* (Warsaw), 13 February 1999.

44. Herbert Dittgen, "Out of Control? Coping with Illegal Immigration in Germany and the United States" (presentation at the annual meeting of the American Political Science Association, Washington, D.C., 28–31 August 1997).

45. *Migration News,* June 1999.

46. Author interview with German customs officials, Frankfurt-Oder, 25 June 1996.

47. Kay Hailbronner et al., "Conclusion: Immigration Admissions and Immigration Controls," in *Immigration Controls: The Search for Workable Policies in Germany and the United States,* ed. Kay Hailbronner et al. (Providence, R.I.: Berghahn, 1997), 205.

local citizens into the immigration control effort. For example, if a taxi driver on the border picks up a foreigner who later turns out to not have proper documents, the driver can be jailed.[48] Germany is in the process of integrating its various bureaucratic surveillance systems (education, welfare, labor, criminal justice) into a central registry in order to monitor more effectively the residency status of all foreigners.[49]

Despite these extensive controls, growing numbers of illegal immigrants are employed throughout the German economy, particularly in such industries as construction and the service sector.[50] It should be stressed, however, that given the more regulated nature of both the German workplace and the broader society, the job magnet is weaker than in the United States, where internal controls remain at token levels. Thus, in the case of immigration, the German border is in a sense much thicker, extending inward into the workplace and outward into neighbors co-opted as buffer zones; the U.S. border remains noticeably thinner—though certainly higher, in the form of fencing, floodlights, and the like.

THE ESCALATION OF POLICING ACROSS THE SPANISH-MOROCCAN BORDER

Along Western Europe's southern frontier has emerged what one observer calls a "European Mexico syndrome—a border-zone where economic, political, cultural, religious and demographic differences accumulate to create a gap between worlds, a zone of confrontation."[51] Analogies have been drawn between the Strait of Gibraltar, which separates Morocco and Spain, and the Río Grande, which divides the United States and Mexico.[52] As on the U.S.-Mexico border, state control over the strait has long been contested by smuggling and other clandestine practices.[53] But in addition to the ten-mile strait between Spain and Morocco, the two countries share a land border because of the Spanish enclave cities of Ceuta and Melilla on the northern Moroccan coast.[54] Thus, Spain has not only

48. *Times* (London), 14 January 1999.
49. Funk, "Control Myths," 15.
50. Bernhard Breuer, "The German Case" (paper presented at Higher Institute of Labour Studies conference on Undocumented Immigrants in the Labour Market: Policy Responses, Brussels, 18–19 January 1996), 11.
51. Jan Nederveen Pieterse, "Fictions of Europe," *Race and Class* 32, no. 3 (1991): 5.
52. Jan Mansvelt Beck and Paolo De Mas, "The Strait of Gibraltar: Europe's Rio Grande?" (paper presented at a symposium on the Mediterranean basin, 28th IGU Congress, the Hague, 7 August 1996).
53. Richard Pennell, "The Geography of Piracy: Northern Morocco in the Mid-Nineteenth Century," *Journal of Historical Geography* 20 (1994): 272–83.
54. Enrique Carabaza and Maximo de Santos, *Melilla y Ceuta: Las Ultimas Colonias* (Madrid: Talasa Ediciones, 1992).

the southernmost point of the EU but also the EU's only land border with Africa.

Marginalized from West European security interests during the Cold War, Spain has become a centerpiece in the new security environment, with the Strait of Gibraltar becoming the "Moat of Fortress Europe."[55] Spain has been building up its border barriers through more guards, new fencing, and better equipment and surveillance technologies. In May 1999, for example, the Spanish government announced that it would spend $160 million on new radar, thermal camera, and night-vision equipment for the Civil Guard along the southern border.[56] The main policing concerns have been the smuggling of migrants and drugs from Morocco, with the former drawing the greatest attention. Some 3,000 migrants have died in the past five years attempting the perilous journey across the strait. Migrants pay smugglers about $1,000 for the trip.[57]

EU policing objectives and Moroccan economic realities are difficult to reconcile. Morocco's two leading generators of foreign exchange are remittances from the 1.4 million Moroccan migrants working in Europe (estimated at $2.4 billion annually)[58] and the export of cannabis products (hashish and marijuana, worth roughly $2 billion annually).[59] Many sub-Saharan Africans also attempt to use Morocco as a springboard to Europe. Through the export of labor and cannabis and involvement in other smuggling activities, Morocco's northern region has become more linked to Europe than to the rest of the country. As one press report put it, "Ask any teenage Moroccan male what his future will be and he will tell you he has three options: to escape across the sea to Europe; become a contraband dealer; or get into the hashish trade and end up either rich or in prison."[60]

According to a 1998 survey, nearly 90 percent of Moroccans in their twenties wanted to leave the country.[61] High unemployment and minimal prospects for upward mobility have been exacerbated by the shocks

55. Henk Driessen, "At the Edge of Europe: Crossing and Marking the Mediterranean Divide," in *Borders, Nations, and States: Frontiers of Sovereignty in the New Europe,* ed. Liam O'Dowd and Thomas M. Wilson (Brookfield, Vt.: Avebury, 1996), 180.

56. *Migration News,* June 1999.

57. *Economist,* 2 January 1999; *Independent,* 20 February 1999.

58. *Financial Times,* 8 August 1995. According to the *Economist,* 2 January 1999, "if Europe were really to stem the flow [of migrants], Morocco might implode."

59. Geopolitical Drug Watch, *The Geopolitics of Drugs* (Boston: Northeastern University Press, 1996). The DEA has noted that "the cultivation and sale of cannabis products provides the economic base for much of northern Morocco." According to INTERPOL, as much as 80 percent of all cannabis confiscated from motorized vehicles in Europe originated in Morocco. See U.S. Drug Enforcement Administration, *Country Brief: Morocco* (Washington, D.C., 1996), 1–3.

60. *Guardian Weekly* (Manchester), 1 March 1998.

61. Reuters World Service, 17 March 1998.

of Morocco's IMF-style economic restructuring program, in place since the 1980s. Researchers have reported that the sweeping market reform program

> has required sharp cutbacks in social spending and in the level of support for export agriculture, with dramatic social consequences: a crisis of the traditional peasantry, internal migration to and overcrowding in urban areas, and a generally deteriorating standard of living. A portion of Morocco's displaced populations is forced to emigrate, often to Spain as illegal workers. . . . Although the wealthy nations support the adjustment strategy that the World Bank and the IMF imposed on Morocco . . . these same nations accept no responsibility for the social consequences of adjustment, including emigration.[62]

The migration exit option, however, has become more difficult as a result of Spain's integration with the rest of Western Europe. The country's southern border is no longer the open door it once was; in a remarkably short period of time, it has been rediscovered and reasserted not simply as a Spanish border but as a European border. As explained by one government report, "National interest as well as the imposed obligations derived from our membership in the EEC [European Economic Community] require us to take measures to articulate a rigorous control at the [southern] border."[63]

Enhanced efforts to secure the southern border, minimally enforced and largely ignored during the Cold War, have gone hand in hand with the Europeanization of Spain. The tightening of Spain's border controls cannot be explained simply as responding to increased illegal border crossings or to EU coercion but rather as integral to the process of shedding a historical inferiority complex and redefining Spain as part of the core of Europe.[64] The rebordering of southern Spain has helped to reaffirm the country's new identity as part of the "inner club." In the new Spain, to be Spanish is to be European, and to be European is to have more secure external borders.

Thus, Spain has not required a great deal of arm-twisting from the EU to police its borders more effectively. Highly self-conscious about its new

62. Colectivo Ioe (Carlos Pereda, Miguel A. de la Prada, and Walter Actis), "Commentary," in *Controlling Immigration,* ed. Wayne Cornelius et al. (Stanford, Calif.: Stanford University Press, 1994), 372.

63. Quoted in Liliana Suarez-Navaz, "Political Economy of the Mediterranean Rebordering: New Ethnicities, New Citizenship," *Stanford Humanities Review* 5, no. 2 (1997): 179.

64. "Napolean's famous statement 'Africa begins at the Pyrenees' has not been forgotten": Cynthia R. Hibbs, "Immigration Policy and the Quotidian Hassles of Being: Foreign Workers in Madrid and San Diego" (master's thesis, University of California at San Diego, 1994), 59.

identification with Europe and its ostracized past during the Franco era, the country has installed stronger border controls to help prove not only to the rest of the EU but to itself that it truly "belongs." In other words, Spain has adopted restrictive EU policing guidelines not simply in the instrumental sense of paying the price of entry into the EU but also as part of redefining what it is to be Spanish in the new Europe.

Cultivating this sense of Europeanness, however, has had to be reconciled with the growing importance of migrant labor in the Spanish economy. Although not historically a destination country for migrants, Spain has become a labor-importing country over the past two decades and immigrants a key ingredient in its economic growth. Indeed, to assure a supply of workers for industries such as agriculture and construction, in late September 1999 Spain signed an agreement with Morocco for the importation of temporary workers. Spain's economic restructuring in the 1980s—including increased labor market segmentation and the growth of the informal economy—created a large demand for cheap unskilled labor in construction, agriculture, and the service sector, even as national unemployment levels remained high. These jobs have often been filled by Africans (especially Moroccans) and Latin Americans who are employed illegally or with temporary work permits. Spain's interior minister, Jaime Mayor Ojeda, has claimed that there are some 600,000 illegal immigrants living in Spain—if true, this would be almost 2 percent of the population.[65] Madrid-based human rights groups estimate that the country has as many as 700,000 illegal workers.[66]

In sharp contrast with much of the rest of Western Europe, noticeably missing from the Spanish political landscape is a major anti-immigrant movement or political party. Parties on the far right have had little public support, given the association in the public's mind between extremism and the Franco regime. As one interior ministry official has noted, "Nowhere on the political spectrum do you find a significant group capable or willing to whip up nativist sentiment."[67] Opinion polls reflect a much higher degree of public tolerance and acceptance of immigrants than is the case among Spain's northern neighbors. In one Spanish opinion poll, for example, only 20 percent of the respondents believed that illegal immigrants should be deported to their home countries.[68] Immigration control remained largely a nonissue until 1985—the year before Spain's entry into the European Community. Until then, the country did not even

65. *Migration News,* February 1998.
66. *Economist,* 2 January 1999.
67. Quoted in Wayne A. Cornelius, "Spain: The Uneasy Transition from Labor Exporter to Labor Importer," in Wayne A. Cornelius et al., *Controlling Immigration,* 360.
68. Ibid., 359.

have a comprehensive immigration law. As part of the new 1985 law (the *Ley de Extranjeria*), employer sanctions were introduced, and the government was given greater power to expel migrants engaged in "illicit activities." Paralleling developments in the United States, a limited legalization program was also adopted (and repeated again in 1991).

As in the U.S. case, Spanish enforcement of workplace controls has remained noticeably lax, and the use of fraudulent working papers has been a growing problem.[69] But in comparison to the United States, Spain has broader societal controls, most evident in mandatory national identification cards and the fact that the homogeneous nature of the society makes it far more difficult for newcomers to "blend in." The police can demand ID cards on the street and selectively target those who are "foreign looking" (i.e., Moroccans and black Africans). Failure to produce proof of legal residence can result in detention and deportation.[70] Moreover, in sharp contrast to the long-established social networks in the United States that have historically facilitated clandestine migration from Mexico, migrant networks in Spain are relatively underdeveloped.

Even though domestic anxiety over immigration has remained minimal in comparison with that in other EU countries and the United States, Spanish politicians have exploited broader European fears of immigration to draw attention to the importance of Spain and the Mediterranean. For example, in the early 1990s Prime Minister Felipe González reportedly planned to give his EU colleagues large photographs of Morocco taken from the Spanish coast. "This is our Río Grande," he wished to remind them. "It's not far. And living standards are four, five, ten times lower on the other side."[71] González has described illegal immigration from North Africa as "the key problem facing Spain and the EC."[72] In 1997 the Spanish government produced an English-language video highlighting its "South Area Action Plan" to beef up its southern border controls. With reassuring images of border officials busy at work—checking for fraudulent documents, arresting illegal immigrants and smugglers, inspecting boats and cars, and building fences—the video's narrator emphasizes how Spain is carrying out its new Schengen obligations.[73]

The year that decisively transformed the practice of illegal immigration and immigration control across Spain's southern border was 1991. After

69. *El Mundo* (Madrid), 7 March 1997.

70. Cornelius, "Spain," 345–46.

71. Ibid., 334.

72. Quoted in Liz Fekete and Frances Webber, *Inside Racist Europe* (London: Institute of Race Relations, 1994), 31.

73. I thank Richard Lewis of the European Commission for sending me this video.

joining Schengen that year, Spain began to impose visa restrictions on its North African neighbors. The impact was immediate and dramatic. Until May 1991, Moroccans and citizens of other Maghreb nations could simply enter Spain legally as tourists and then work illegally. When it became public knowledge that a new visa requirement was to be imposed, law enforcement officials in the Spanish port city of Algeciras were overwhelmed by the number of Moroccans trying to get in; thousands were turned back.[74]

As soon as the visa restriction took effect, migrants turned to various clandestine entry methods, including stowing away on ships, working on Spanish fishing vessels and then sneaking into the country when they docked for unloading, and using fraudulent visas.[75] As elsewhere, migrants also turned to professional smugglers to transport them across the strait in small, overcrowded boats (called *pateras*). The Moroccan port city of Tangier, which had for centuries been a center of smuggling from Africa to Europe, emerged as a bustling market for migrant-smuggling travel services. In order to pay for the expensive crossing (estimated at $700–$1,000 per person), some migrants would carry packages of hashish—which in turn reinforced the popular perception in Spain of a close association between illegal immigration and drug trafficking.[76]

While numerically the least significant method of clandestine entry, the rising *patera* traffic across the strait attracted enormous public and media attention. There was almost daily media coverage in 1991–92, with the press even describing those who attempted the illegal crossing as "wetbacks" (borrowing the term long applied to Mexican migrants crossing the Río Grande).[77] Thus, once largely ignored as little more than a popular destination point for sun-seeking vacationers, Spain's southern border was suddenly placed in the European political spotlight, and the rising numbers of migrants drowned and washed up on Spain's southern beaches made headlines in the national and foreign press.

These dramatic images prompted the EU to pressure Spain for more forceful border controls, and Spain in turn joined the EU in pressuring Morocco for the same. Spain enhanced its policing apparatus, creating a special force to control illegal immigration at the border. In 1992 it deployed new patrol ships with electronic detection equipment and helicopters with infrared cameras and high-powered spotlights. At the same time,

74. Driessen, "At the Edge of Europe."
75. A forged visa bought in Tangier reportedly costs about $3,000: *Economist*, 2 January 1999.
76. Hibbs, "Immigration Policy," 44.
77. Driessen, "At the Edge of Europe," 180.

Spain threatened to cancel trade agreements unless Morocco clamped down on the clandestine crossings.[78]

Securing Morocco's cooperation in the antismuggling effort was facilitated by the Moroccan government's desire for a new fishing rights agreement with Spain and closer economic ties to Western Europe. After the Moroccan government assured officials that it would tighten controls on drug and migrant smuggling, in December 1992 the EU indicated it would negotiate with Morocco one of the closest partnership treaties ever drawn up between the union and a non-European state.[79] The EU subsequently pushed forward with plans for a free-trade zone with Morocco, which some officials even referred to as "Europe's Mexico."[80]

As part of the effort to impress his northern neighbors, the king of Morocco declared in 1992 a "war on drugs and illegal immigration."[81] Ordering the Justice Ministry to draw up "a judicial arsenal providing heavier penalties for drug trafficking and clandestine emigration," he told his cabinet ministers and security chiefs to "wage an implacable and ceaseless struggle against the two scourges."[82] The crackdown included a militarization of border controls, with Royal Army soldiers posted at observation posts along the Mediterranean coast and the Royal Navy carrying out regular patrols.[83] Some 5,000 soldiers were deployed to the northern region, hundreds of roadblocks and checkpoints established, and round-the-clock sea and air patrols initiated. "Our war against the smugglers is nothing less than draconian," claimed Morocco's interior minister in early 1993; it had "seriously affected the livelihoods of about 3 million Moroccan citizens."[84] In 1994 the fight against drugs and the task of border control were said to have cost more than $100 million (over 5 percent of the national budget).[85]

Within a short period of time, the most visible and publicized form of migrant smuggling, the use of *pateras* to cross the strait, was significantly reduced. Many of the smuggling operations based in Tangier were either broken up or pushed further underground and out of sight. A new police

78. *International Herald Tribune,* 24 November 1995.

79. Driessen, "At the Edge of Europe," 195.

80. *Christian Science Monitor,* 27 January 1993.

81. Beck and De Mas, "Strait of Gibraltar," 19.

82. Reuters Library Report, 7 October 1992.

83. U.S. Department of State, *International Narcotics Control Strategy Report* (Washington, D.C., 1997).

84. Quoted in *Washington Post,* 23 January 1993.

85. Kingdom of Morocco, *White Paper: Moroccan General Policy in the Area of the Fight against Drug Trafficking and for the Economic Development of the Northern Provinces* (Rabat: Kingdom of Morocco, November 1994).

chief was appointed, and immigrants from sub-Saharan Africa suspected of planning to cross the strait were rounded up.[86] One smuggler in Tangier noted that "before the surveillance, it was like a travel agency, and people built boats especially designed to hold maybe 12 or 15 people. But now it is more difficult . . . because of the patrols."[87] The incentives for the crackdown were not difficult to decipher. As one news report explained, the Moroccan government was "desperate to impress Europe with its measures to stop illegal immigration as part of an effort to strengthen ties with the European Union."[88]

Cannabis smuggling, however, was more deeply entrenched in the local economy and thus continued to flourish. Indeed, cannabis production reached record levels in the years following the 1992–93 crackdown, making Morocco the largest cannabis supplier to Europe.[89] Although many smaller exporters and producers were eliminated, the market position of the more sophisticated trafficking organizations expanded. The International Criminal Police Organization (INTERPOL) was nevertheless pleased with the Moroccan government's display of force, praising the country's new commitment to the UN convention on illicit drugs, which Morocco had signed in 1992.[90]

In comparison with the heated U.S. drug policy discourse over Mexico and other drug-exporting countries, the EU's reaction to the rapid growth of the Moroccan cannabis trade—estimated to have increased tenfold since the 1980s—has been muted. Indeed, many EU member states have preferred to verbally assault the Netherlands for its liberal drug policies while largely overlooking Morocco. The EU's silence is explained by a number of complementary factors. First, West European countries have been less prone than the United States to blame drug-exporting countries for their own domestic drug consumption problems, and given the tolerant policies toward cannabis consumption in much of the EU, blaming Morocco would be doubly difficult. Second, the EU has been wary of overly offending the Moroccan government, since Morocco is considered an important buffer against Islamic fundamentalism and the more volatile countries in the region (especially Algeria). A third and perhaps more cynical explanation is that the EU has recognized cannabis production as Morocco's leading generator of export revenue and therefore an integral component of Moroccan stability. Indeed, cannabis export, which has

86. Driessen, "At the Edge of Europe," 195.
87. Quoted in *Christian Science Monitor*, 3 November 1995.
88. Ibid.
89. Geopolitical Drug Watch, *World Geopolitics of Drugs*.
90. *Financial Times*, 8 August 1995.

provided the economic base for the northern Rif region, has in a sense served as an indirect form of immigration control, offering a domestic underground alternative to illegal migration. As one EU official warned, the danger to be avoided was "people running down the mountains and, instead of stopping in the towns, swimming across the Mediterranean."[91]

Tellingly, the Moroccan government's second high-profile antidrug campaign of the 1990s was sparked not by political pressure and public criticism from the EU but rather by highly embarrassing media exposure. In 1995 a confidential study, sponsored by the European Commission and leaked to the press, asserted that the Moroccan government was protecting the drug trade and that the crackdown earlier in the decade had been little more than window dressing.[92] The report's extensive media coverage in Europe could not have come at a more diplomatically sensitive time for Morocco, for the government was in the final stages of negotiating a free-trade agreement with the EU (which was signed on 11 November 1995).[93]

Outraged by such public embarrassment, the Moroccan government launched a new and expanded attack on the cannabis trade. Some of the most conspicuous traffickers in Tangier and Tétouan were arrested, as was a former governor of Tangier.[94] Nineteen customs officials—almost the entire senior staff of Morocco's customs office—were charged with fraud and smuggling, including the head of the government's campaign against fraud and the director of customs.[95] A number of shipping companies in Tangier were charged with smuggling hashish in their Europe-bound cargoes of fresh produce and frozen fish.[96] The cleansing campaign, although designed to improve Morocco's international image, also reinforced the government's already powerful grip over Moroccan society. As one observer put it, "The key thing is that the measures being taken in Morocco are not aimed at ending the drugs trade. They are aimed at strengthening the power of the key ministries."[97]

The tensions between EU political goals and local economic realities are sharpest in the Spanish enclave cities of Ceuta and Melilla along Morocco's northern coast. It is here that the southern edge of the EU is most visibly marked and contested. These two enclaves, established as city fortresses after the expulsion of the Moors from Spain some 500 years ago, originally served as military outposts to provide advance warning of an Is-

---

91. Quoted in ibid.
92. *Guardian*, 4 November 1995; *Sunday Telegraph Limited*, 3 December 1995.
93. Geopolitical Drug Watch, *World Geopolitics of Drugs*.
94. *New York Times*, 16 August 1996.
95. *United Press International*, 16 February 1996.
96. *New York Times*, 16 August 1996.
97. Quoted in *Observer* (London), 16 June 1996.

lamic attack. They have now become strategic policing outposts at the southern perimeter of Western Europe. As explained by Enrique Beaumud, the Spanish government's representative in Melilla, "We can't let Ceuta and Melilla become trampolines to get into Spain and Europe."[98]

In Ceuta the EU has helped to fund a road and fence construction project intended to insulate the city from Morocco.[99] When the plan was first conceived, the fence was dubbed Europe's new Berlin Wall.[100] As explained by Roberto Franks, spokesperson for the Spanish government in Ceuta, "Without doubt this is the southern frontier of the Europe of Schengen. We have a whole continent to the south of us. It is increasingly evident that this wall is necessary."[101] Spanish military personnel began the construction in 1995.[102] The ten-foot-high, five-mile-long double fence has sensors to detect illegal crossings, thirty closed-circuit TV cameras, and high-intensity floodlights; it is patrolled by the army, the police, and the Civil Guard.[103] Similarly, in Melilla—where the only separation from Morocco used to be a coil of barbed wire[104]—the EU has helped finance the construction of a double fence along the city's six-mile border with Morocco. These ten-foot barriers, with their watchtowers, video cameras, and optic sensors, cost around $10 million.[105] Dozens of Spanish guards are stationed every 50 yards.

The walling off of Ceuta and Melilla is more apparent than real, however, masking the fact that the economies of the two cities depend on their retaining porous borders. Thousands of Moroccans enter Ceuta and Melilla every day (legally and illegally) for local business, and within this flow is a smaller number of Africans hoping to use the cities as an entry point to the Spanish mainland. "Of the 15,000 people who come in [legally every day] there are always some who get through illegally," acknowledged Luis Manuel Aznar, a spokesman for the Spanish government in Ceuta.[106] Moroccans caught without proper papers are simply sent back across the border, but the Moroccan government generally refuses to accept persons

98. Reuters, 23 August 1998.

99. As of January 2000 the fence had not been completed, with the Spanish government estimating that it would be done by mid-year. The final cost for completion was expected to be $60 million (roughly 25 percent coming from the EU)—far higher than initially planned. George Stolz, "Europe's Back Doors," *Atlantic Monthly* 285, no. 1 (2000): 26–33.

100. *European* (London), 20 July 1998.

101. *Statewatch* 5, no. 6 (1995): 1.

102. *El País* (Madrid), 20 October 1995.

103. *Independent* (London), 20 February 1999.

104. *Christian Science Monitor*, 27 July 1998; Reuters, 23 August 1998.

105. Dawn/Guardian News Service, 30 June 1998.

106. Quoted in *Sunday Telegraph* (London), 26 July 1998.

who are from other parts of Africa.[107] Some of these then apply for political asylum and are held in cramped detention facilities.[108] To reduce crowding in the camps, migrants are eventually sent to the Spanish mainland, where they can disappear into the vast informal economy while the government is reviewing their cases. Thus, although only about 4 percent of asylum applicants are accepted, applying for asylum can still provide a back door into Spain.[109] Since late 1996, the Spanish government has also been selectively handing out special work and residency permits as an alternative to reviewing asylum requests. Consequently, more and more migrants are simply opting to wait for a work permit rather than apply for asylum. This situation, one observer suggests, has transformed Ceuta and Melilla into "a sort of waiting room" in which the government can "screen for able-bodied potential workers."[110]

As to the double fence being built around Ceuta, people were soon going over,[111] underneath,[112] through,[113] or around[114] it. Local economic realities encourage lax enforcement. Most of the crossers simply enter

107. In a 1992 bilateral agreement the Moroccan government agreed to take back non-Moroccan nationals who had entered Spain through Moroccan territory. In practice, however, very few are actually accepted; many non-Moroccan migrants "lose" or hide their documents, making it difficult for Spanish authorities to determine their country of origin. Author interview with Spanish police officials, Ceuta, Spain, 26 May 1997.

108. More than 16,000 sub-Saharan Africans were arrested in Melilla and Ceuta in 1997: *Migration News*, August 1998. In 1997 the Spanish army was sent to Melilla to assist the Civil Guard in handling riots that erupted at an immigration detention center. The new fencing around Melilla, Spain's Interior Ministry has argued, will make it possible for the army to withdraw: Dawn/Guardian News Service, 30 June 1998.

109. *Independent*, 20 February 1998; *Economist*, 2 January 1999.

110. Stolz, "Europe's Back Doors."

111. Climbing over both fences reportedly takes a little more than a minute: *European* (London), 20 July 1998.

112. On 26 May 1997, I was given a tour of the new fence by Ceuta police officials. As the police car I was riding in turned a corner, people were entering through a large drainage tunnel underneath the fence in front of us. The Civil Guardsmen nearby were standing aside, but when they noticed our car, they jumped to attention and started pushing the crossers back. Presumably, once our car had passed, the fence again became a door rather than a barrier (the Associated Press reported on 17 August 1999 that the forty drainage tunnels running under the fence are now being blocked). A few minutes later, this scene repeated itself near the port of entry. As we approached, a local smuggler was attempting to cross into Morocco with his goods, but the Moroccan official on duty stood in the way. When the smuggler turned back to try a different entry point, he was blocked by the Spanish Civil Guardsman because our police car had entered the scene. Thus, the smuggler was momentarily caught in a limbo between Spanish and Moroccan law enforcement, having to wait patiently until one side or the other opened up.

113. Border guards have spent much of their time repairing holes in the fence: *European*, 20 July 1998.

114. People can wade or float on inner tubes around the end of the fence.

Ceuta to purchase Spanish goods and then smuggle them back across the border. Even though local residents from the surrounding province of Tétouan are allowed to enter Ceuta for the day without obtaining a visa, many opt to go back and forth across the fence, thus avoiding Moroccan authorities at the port of entry. Ceuta's economic reliance on the thriving contraband trade is an open secret—not officially denied but generally left politely unmentioned.[115] Since Morocco has no customs service at the Ceuta port of entry, the flow of goods into Morocco through Ceuta is by definition composed entirely of smuggling. Indeed, giant Spanish ware-houses have been built right next to the border fence to facilitate the con-traband business.

Given the magnitude of the smuggling trade *into* Morocco (reported to be worth around $2 billion annually),[116] some Moroccans find it hypocrit-ical for Europeans to expect tighter controls on the smuggling of drugs and migrants out of Morocco. Mohammed Abbasy, past president of the Tangier Chamber of Commerce and Industry, has stated that "no Moroc-can finds it tolerable for Europe to ask Morocco to fight clandestine emi-gration and drug trafficking while a neighboring country like Spain allows its police and customs officers to stand by as merchandise flows illegally toward Morocco. These days, Sebta [Ceuta] and Melilla survive exclusively on contraband and the time has come to put an end to this situation."[117]

Yet Morocco largely tolerates the influx of Spanish contraband. Some-times Moroccan border guards passively observe the smuggling, some-times they charge a fee, and sometimes they confiscate smuggled goods. How open the border is to the contraband trade varies from month to month, week to week, day to day, and even hour to hour; the continuously renegotiated process functions as an informal method of regulating the contraband business. But a serious and long-lasting crackdown would un-dermine local economies on both sides and sour cross-border relations.[118]

The reality is that both Spain and Morocco have in many ways benefited from the smuggling economy. The northern regions of Morocco sur-rounding Ceuta and Melilla depend on the illegal export of cannabis; the much-needed hard currency it generates helps to sustain the importa-tion of contraband manufactured goods from Spain; and the contraband trade into northern Morocco, in turn, helps to launder the profits of the

115. When I asked Ceuta police officials what the most important sectors of the local economy were, they did not mention smuggling. But when I asked them how important smuggling was, they all admitted that it was the leading economic activity in the city. Author interview with Spanish police officials, Ceuta, Spain, 26 May 1997.

116. Geopolitical Drug Watch, *The Geopolitics of Drugs,* 94.

117. Quoted in ibid., 95.

118. Author interview with Spanish police officials, Ceuta, Spain, 26 May 1997.

drug trade.[119] Some diplomatic sources have estimated that a third of the legal goods on sale in Morocco have been smuggled into the country by the same people who smuggle cannabis products out.[120]

Thus, even as Ceuta and Melilla have become new policing outposts for the EU, they are also deeply enmeshed in a clandestine form of cross-border interdependence that runs counter to the EU's stated law enforcement objectives. Indeed, the more profitable the smuggling of drugs is for Morocco, the more profitable the smuggling of contraband goods is for Spain's two enclave cities. As one Spanish official has candidly put it, the contraband economy and the drug economy are "linked like a chain."[121]

An examination of policing trends across two external borders of the European Union helps illuminate what is and is not distinctive about the U.S.-Mexico experience. Together, these EU borders and the U.S.-Mexico border represent critical fault lines—but also bridges—between rich and poor regions. In each case there has been a growing tension between the policy goals of facilitating desirable cross-border economic flows and deterring undesirable flows.

Beyond these basic similarities, however, there are crucial variations. One striking difference between the expanding U.S. and German immigration control efforts is that U.S. controls have focused almost exclusively on the border itself, whereas German controls have extended much deeper into society. Methods politically inconceivable in the United States (national identity cards, extensive workplace and societal regulation) are taken for granted in Germany. And methods politically unthinkable in Germany (extensive border fencing, floodlights, military assistance) receives broad political support in the United States. Moreover, whereas Germany's lifting of visa restrictions for its immediate eastern neighbors has helped secure their cooperation in controlling migrant smuggling, at least for now it is difficult to imagine U.S. officials even contemplating a similar move to secure Mexico's cooperation. Most important, when Poland and other bordering states are integrated into the European Union in the near future, the focus of policing will shift eastward. In the current political context, it remains inconceivable that the United States would fully open the border with Mexico in exchange for fortifying Mexico's *southern* border.

Spain has combined aspects of both U.S. and German immigration control strategies. It shares the minimalist U.S. approach toward workplace enforcement and has built the kind of high-profile fencing favored along the U.S.-Mexico border. And Spain has certainly become more like

119. Geopolitical Drug Watch, *The Geopolitics of Drugs,* 94.
120. *Observer* (London), 16 June 1996.
121. Author interview, Spanish Ministry of the Interior, Madrid, 28 May 1997.

the United States in imposing visa requirements on its southern neighbors. Unlike the United States and similar to Germany, however, Spain has relied on national identity cards. Also similar to Germany, Spain has justified the tightening of external borders not as a unilateral reassertion of territorial sovereignty but as a strategy embedded within a broader European framework for "pooling sovereignty." In the U.S., by contrast, it is precisely the image of defending national sovereignty that has been projected through the escalation of border policing.

One reason for this difference is that the images projected by border policing have been directed toward different audiences in each of the three countries. On the one hand, since the tightening of Spanish border controls primarily reflects EU rather than domestic politics, the main audience has been other EU member states. To the extent that erecting more formidable-looking border barriers appeals to a domestic audience, it has had less to do with anxiety over immigrants and drugs than with expressing and reinforcing Spain's new identity and importance as a European "insider." The escalation of U.S. border policing, on the other hand, has been primarily aimed at reassuring a nervous domestic audience that law enforcement is doing more to secure the border. Germany represents a kind of middle case: state officials work to appease and impress both internal and external audiences.

The heightened border-policing efforts on the other sides of these borders—in Morocco, Poland, and Mexico—have largely reflected external political pressures and expectations and those countries' larger priority of encouraging closer economic ties to their wealthier neighbors. Thus, their primary audience has been external. The methods used to impress this audience have varied, however. For example, Morocco has deployed military forces to confront both drug and migrant smuggling across the Strait of Gibraltar. Mexico would not even consider such a response to inhibit Mexican citizens from illegally crossing into the United States (freedom of exit, Mexican officials make sure to remind their American counterparts, is guaranteed in the constitution) yet has gone further than Morocco and most other countries in militarizing its drug control campaign. And although Mexico, Morocco, and Poland have all faced external scrutiny in the area of drug control, the drug issue has been noticeably more divisive and politicized in U.S.-Mexico relations. It is immigration control, not drug control, that has primarily propelled the escalation of German and Spanish border policing.

CHAPTER SEVEN

Borders Restated

Even as old border barriers have been torn down, new ones have been rapidly built up. The perceived new threats are not military invaders but law evaders, with the smuggling of drugs and migrants topping the list of policy concerns. This has been especially evident along the territorial fault lines between lands of wealth and lands of poverty, most notably the southern border of the United States and the southern and eastern borders of the European Union. During the past decade, policing illegal flows across these borders has been transformed from a low-priority and low-maintenance activity into a high-profile campaign attracting growing political attention.

The purpose of this book has been to explain this sharp escalation of border enforcement and its distinct trajectories across place and policing missions. Focusing primarily on the U.S.-Mexico experience, my explanation for escalation has stressed the role of policy feedback effects and the primacy of image management and symbolic politics for state actors. Escalation provided a political mechanism for coping with the often perverse and unintended consequences of past policy choices and generated substantial rewards for lawmakers and law enforcers by communicating a commitment to territorial integrity and projecting an image of territorial authority. At the same time, the persistent failures and negative side effects of escalation only fueled calls to escalate even further.

The unprecedented effort to police the boundary between the United States and Mexico is particularly striking because it came at the same time that the two countries were embracing a common vision of a border-free North American economic space. The retreat of the state in the name of market liberalization has been matched by the reassertion of state policing in the name of market criminalization. The simultaneous creation of a borderless economy and a barricaded border may seem paradoxical and has certainly created some awkward policy tensions and dilemmas. Yet as I have stressed, part of the political project of turning the border into a more expansive economic bridge has also involved making it at least appear to be a more formidable police barrier. As a result, the border has become both more blurred and more sharply demarcated than ever before.

For those state actors who have helped orchestrate the rolling-back of the state to promote the economic opening of borders, there is nothing paradoxical about also rolling forward the policing apparatus of the state to patrol borders more intensively. A liberalizing state is not necessarily a less interventionist state. Thus, for example, when President Clinton declared the "end of the era of big government" in his 1996 State of the Union address, he also announced the appointment of a military general to lead a reinvigorated antidrug campaign and stressed that his administration was the first to get serious about securing the nation's borders against illegal immigration. In this case, "reinventing government" was less about reducing the regulatory state than about retooling and redeploying it.

The U.S.-Mexico border is in many ways distinctive: it is the most heavily traveled land crossing in the world and also one of the most heavily fortified. Yet in some respects it represents the changing relationship between rich and poor countries generally. It was not so long ago that third-world resistance to the first world's promotion of economic liberalism was a major source of international friction.[1] Since the debt crisis of the 1980s, however, most developing countries have embraced the tenets of economic liberalism through sweeping market reforms, IMF-style structural adjustment programs, and greater integration with the global economy. Perhaps ironically, it is now the advanced industrialized states that remain most resistant to economic liberalism, building up their protective walls against two of the developing world's leading exports: drugs and migrant labor. As the source of these high-demand exports, many poor countries have in essence taken literally the advice of Western free-market proponents by engaging in those economic activities that provide them with a comparative advantage and market niche. In many cases, these underground exit options are crucial sources of employment and revenue, helping to cushion the painful shocks of the market-based economic restructuring process. Imposing higher tariffs in the form of more intensive policing has helped to deny but not defy this sobering reality. The degree of conflict between

1. Stephen Krasner, *Structural Conflict: The Third World against Global Liberalism* (Berkeley: University of California Press, 1985).

many rich and poor countries will no doubt continue to depend significantly on how they cope politically with this clandestine side of their economic relationship.

BORDER NARRATIVES

The story line of border policing can take various forms, directing attention to some facts and not to others and offering an interpretation of those facts. The narrative that dominates much of the official policy debate in the United States, for example, characterizes borders as under siege by clandestine transnational activities, with the smuggling of drugs and migrants drawing most of the attention. It is a nostalgic narrative: it assumes that borders once constituted effective shelter. For those who consider them now "out of control," the narrative provides a rallying cry to "regain control." As one senior State Department official has urged: "Every country must develop tough new policies aimed at restoring its borders so that they are again meaningful protection against criminals, drugs, weapons, and illegal immigration."[2] To dramatize the gravity of the border problem, Senator John Kerry (D-Mass.) even draws an analogy between old and new threats: "Historically, many wars began with border incidents, one country probing the protective membrane of another. In the war with the transnational criminal organizations, our borders are flouted regularly, whether by smugglers carrying narcotics or trading in the most precious and pathetic commodity of all—human beings."[3] Although a comparison between military threats and transnational crime threats does more to inflame the passions than enlighten the mind, it does reflect the new sense of urgency that has gripped some policy circles.

This popular border narrative contains important truths. Border laws *are* constantly violated, sometimes violently, in ways that mock the territorial credibility of the state. The narrative ultimately conceals more than it reveals, however. For one thing, it is misleading. Characterizing policing efforts as simply a defensive response to an expanding smuggling challenge glosses over the ways in which state practices have powerfully conditioned and even encouraged smuggling (often unintentionally) and conveniently draws attention away from the enormous domestic consumer demand that provides a powerful magnet for smuggling.

2. Jonathan M. Winer, deputy assistant secretary of state for international law enforcement matters, "Anti-narcotics and Money Laundering Enforcement: Core Components of Maintaining Democracy" (paper presented to the Latin American Studies Association, Washington, D.C., 28 September 1995), 11–12.

3. John Kerry, *The New War: The Web of Crime That Threatens America's Security* (New York: Simon & Schuster, 1997), 149.

The dominant border narrative is also incomplete; it suffers from historical amnesia. Urgent appeals to "restore borders" forget the fact that, with rare exceptions, the deterrent effect of borders has long been more imaginary than real.[4] Indeed, from a broader historical perspective, the development of comprehensive border controls is relatively recent. And it is the very existence and enforcement of such controls, after all, which has made it necessary for many border crossers to try to circumvent them. In other words, rather than simply reflecting the impotence of the state, clandestine cross-border flows also reflect the power of the state to determine who and what have legal territorial access.

The border narrative offered in this book suggests that the escalation of policing has been less about deterring than about image crafting. Judging border controls primarily in terms of their technical success or failure to meet the stated instrumental goal of deterrence misses much of what these territorial practices are all about. Border enforcement is about deterrence, but it is also about propping up state claims to territorial authority and symbolically reaffirming the traditional political boundaries of an "imagined community." As Timothy Mitchell reminds us, "Setting up and policing a frontier involves a variety of fairly modern social practices—continuous barbed-wire fencing, passports, immigration laws, inspectors, currency controls, and so on. These mundane arrangements . . . help manufacture an almost transcendental entity, the nation state."[5] From this perspective, statecraft is not just about power politics and deploying material resources. It is also about image politics and deploying symbolic resources. State power is based on physical capabilities and coercion, but it is also fundamentally based on legitimacy and its symbolic representation.[6]

This conception of statecraft, rooted in a sociological understanding of laws and their enforcement, has informed much of my narrative of border policing. Laws are not only forms of direct social control but also carriers of meanings: "The police" says Joseph Gusfield, "represent the visible presence of those meanings, meanings that are always somewhat fictive and problematic, but which are nevertheless maintained." Laws establish and maintain moral boundaries: "The public drama of law provides the ex-

4. See Janice Thomson and Stephen Krasner, "Global Transactions and the Consolidation of Sovereignty," in *Global Changes and Theoretical Challenges: Approaches to World Politics for the 1990s,* ed. Ernst-Otto Czempiel and James N. Rosenau (Lexington, Mass.: Lexington Books, 1989), 198, which rightly points out that there never has been a "golden age" of state control.

5. Timothy Mitchell, "The Limits of the State: Beyond Statist Approaches and Their Critics," *American Political Science Review* 85, no. 1 (1991): 91. On the construction of national identities, see Benedict Anderson, *Imagined Communities* (London: Verso, 1991).

6. Roger Friedland and Robert A. Alford, "Bringing Society Back In: Symbols, Practices, and Institutional Contradictions," in *The New Institutionalism in Organizational Analysis,* ed. Walter W. Powell and Paul J. DiMaggio (Chicago: University of Chicago Press, 1991), 238.

pectations and perceptions of what is normal and acclaimed and what is deviant and condemned. It tells us what is publicly admissible."[7] The symbolic function of law is nowhere more apparent than in the criminal justice system. Prohibiting and punishing are "signifying practices" that communicate where authority is located, how order and community are to be maintained, and where to expect threats.[8]

From this view, border policing should be seen not simply as a strategy of deterrence but as a ritualistic performance.[9] When the failures of the deterrence effort lead to a performance crisis, the performers save face by promising a bigger and better show. The audience may cheer or jeer, but the credibility of the performance is rarely seriously questioned. An effective performance, however, requires much more than tough talk and promises. As the U.S.-Mexico border experience illustrates, the political and bureaucratic allure of enhanced law enforcement is that it has delivered perceptually appealing and symbolically useful indicators of state activity: smugglers arrested, drugs seized, and so on. And in the case of immigration control, the crackdown on illegal crossings along the most visible stretches of the border has erased politically embarrassing images of chaos and replaced them with comforting images of order. The border control offensive has successfully decreased the visibility, even though not necessarily the number, of illegal border crossings, while increasing the visibility of policing.

Unfortunately, however, visible signs of state resolve create the conditions for further escalation: smugglers who respond with more sophisticated border-crossing methods provide a rationale for even more intensive and extensive policing. Those officials charged with the task of securing the border can thus simultaneously praise their enforcement progress *and* point to the emergence of a more formidable enforcement problem— which in turn justifies more funding. Escalation, in other words, feeds on itself.

And so the border game of law enforcement and law evasion continues. The official indicators used to evaluate the game are ambiguous and therefore easy to manipulate. Almost any outcome (for example, either a decrease or an increase in arrests and seizures) can be politically inter-

7. Joseph Gusfield, *The Culture of Public Problems: Drinking-Driving and the Symbolic Order* (Chicago: University of Chicago Press, 1981), 159, 181.

8. David Garland, *Punishment in Modern Society* (Chicago: University of Chicago Press, 1990).

9. This view reinforces the conclusion of James G. March and Johan P. Olsen, *Rediscovering Institutions: The Organizational Basis of Politics* (New York: Free Press, 1984), 735, that analysis of the state should more fully incorporate a recognition of "the ways in which political life is organized around the development of meaning through symbols, rituals and ceremonies."

preted both as a sign of law enforcement progress and as a sign that much more enforcement is needed. Many official objectives—such as increasing "interagency coordination," improving "bilateral cooperation," and "disrupting" smuggling patterns—are so vaguely defined that they defy precise measurement. The game score is often recorded in the form of "body counts"—number of smugglers captured, amount of drugs destroyed, and so on. Many of the indicators used as evidence of law enforcement success (such as the higher fees smugglers charge the migrants) also benefit the smugglers. And many of the measures emphasized by the law enforcers to show they have been playing hard (more drugs interdicted, more smugglers apprehended) may actually indicate more smuggling. Yet rather than challenging the indicators used to evaluate the game, most policymakers simply push for playing harder. Their public statements have more to do with reaffirming a moral commitment to staying in the game than with any fundamental appraisal of the logic of the game itself.

BORDER LESSONS

Border narratives have prescriptive implications. Lessons drawn from the narrative determine what policy options are considered legitimate and which ones are dismissed or ignored. Policy analysis and policy prescription, therefore, are never as divorced as many would like to believe. The border narrative that informs much of the Washington policy debate, for instance, defines the problems of drugs and illegal immigration primarily as combinations of externally driven threats and inadequate defenses to repel them. As Representative John L. Mica (R-Fla.) has put it in the case of drugs: "The correlation between a loose border and human misery in this country is obvious."[10] The policy solution thus seems equally obvious: tighten border controls. And when doing so fails to achieve adequate deterrence, then tighten some more.

This logic has led some public officials to push for further militarization of the border. In June 1999, for example, the House of Representatives endorsed an amendment to the defense bill that would authorize dispatching 10,000 troops to the southwestern border to curb the influx of drugs and illegal immigrants. Representative James Traficant (D-Ohio), the sponsor of the measure, argued that "the number one security threat facing America, the weak link, is our border."[11] Other prominent politi-

10. Statement of Representative John L. Mica, House Subcommittee on Criminal Justice, Drug Policy, and Human Resources, Committee on Government Reform, *Examining the Drug Threat along the Southwest Border,* 106th Cong., 1st sess., 24 September 1999.
11. Quoted in Associated Press, 11 June 1999.

cal voices, such as Patrick Buchanan, have proposed building an enormous border wall patrolled by the military.[12] Although opposing such plans, administration officials have nevertheless promoted their own version of escalation: more border agents, more and better inspection and surveillance technologies, more drug control collaboration with Mexico. In short, rather than questioning whether or not to escalate, the policy debate has largely revolved around how and how much to escalate.

But continued escalation, although it may be the path of least political and bureaucratic resistance, merely chases the symptoms of the deeper problem: the seemingly insatiable domestic appetite for mind-altering substances and cheap migrant labor. The unwillingness to confront the demand side squarely means that the flow of drugs and migrants will likely keep going around, underneath, or through the border defenses—assuring a thriving business for both law enforcers and law-evading smugglers.

Domestic measures to curb the demand for drugs (treatment, education, and prevention) take a distant back seat to supply-focused law enforcement.[13] Of the nearly $18 billion the federal government annually spends to combat drugs, about two-thirds focuses on supply reduction and only one third on demand. This is certainly not based on cost-effectiveness. For example, a 1994 RAND study found that $34 million invested in treatment reduces cocaine use as much as does $366 million invested in border interdiction or $783 million invested in source-country programs.[14] Efforts to interdict the supply have had little impact on the domestic price and availability of drugs, and even dramatic improvements in interdiction are unlikely to change this fact.[15] An abundant supply and the high profits of the illicit trade make drug seizures a relatively small cost of doing business for smugglers. The heart of the nation's drug problem is chronic drug use; it is therefore first and foremost a public health rather than a law

12. The idea of such a massive border barrier prompted the *New York Times* to get estimates from various companies on how much it would cost. Estimates ranged from $166.8 million for a basic chain-link fence to $45.2 billion for a twenty-five-feet-high and twenty-feet-thick at the base concrete structure similar to the Great Wall of China. The final bill, it jokingly reported, would depend on whether the contractor hired legal or illegal workers.

13. Representative John Conyers (D-Mich.) has explained the political logic in Congress: "Drug education and treatment have gained a name as a wimp activity. If you favor these things, you're a softy. When these proposals come up in Congress most members want to know, before they vote, which one is toughest? It's sort of, 'I don't know if this is going to work, but nobody is going to blame me for not being tough'": quoted in *New York Times,* 28 July 1992.

14. Cited in Council on Foreign Relations, *Task Force Report: Rethinking International Drug Control* (Washington, D.C., 1997), 55.

15. Peter Reuter, "Quantity Illusions and Paradoxes of Drug Interdiction: Federal Investigation into Vice Policy," *Law and Contemporary Problems* 51, no. 1 (1988): 233–52.

enforcement problem.[16] Roughly 4 million people in the United States are hard-core drug users and, although representing only about 20 percent of the total drug-using population, consume the bulk of the drug supply. Washington's approach to reducing demand is driven primarily by punitive measures: large numbers of drug users are locked up on possession charges, only to find that drugs are easily available in the nation's vast prison system.[17]

The scant attention paid to the demand side is even more transparent in the case of immigration control. Of all advanced industrialized countries the United States imposes the toughest penalties on the smuggling of migrants and related activities yet is among the most lenient with those who employ them.[18] While the policy debate is dominated by the discourse of "stopping the flood of immigrants" and "controlling the border," only a negligible portion of the INS budget is devoted to enforcing the country's anemic employer sanctions laws, and Congress has yet to approve a forgery-resistant employment documentation system.[19] Equally important, existing workplace rules (minimum wages; overtime pay; environmental, health, and safety regulations) are only loosely enforced. Systematic enforcement of these rules would make it more difficult for employers to engage in the extreme exploitation of workers and would thus undermine their most important incentive to hire illegal labor. However modest the impact might be, an emphasis on workplace controls and raising labor standards would go much further toward weeding out the root of the problem than do tightened border controls. A policy turn away from the border, however, is politically difficult, since it would no doubt cause an allergic reaction among employers who have long been accustomed to minimal state intervention. As one INS official bluntly puts it, "The border is easy money politically. But the interior is a political minefield."[20]

Some readers might draw a more cynical, Machiavellian lesson from this book: border escalation may be a march of folly, but it nevertheless remains the optimal policy path precisely because it offers a perceptually

16. On the public health approach to drugs, see Eva Bertram, Morris Blachman, Kenneth Sharpe, and Peter Andreas, *Drug War Politics: The Price of Denial* (Berkeley: University of California Press, 1996).

17. Drug-related arrests have skyrocketed since the 1980s and currently number more than 1.5 million a year—nearly 700,000 for the sale or possession of marijuana alone. The United States has the highest incarceration rate among advanced industrialized countries, partly thanks to harsh mandatory minimum sentencing for drug law violators.

18. *Trafficking in Migrants Quarterly Bulletin*, September 1996.

19. Tellingly, the INS did not request more inspectors to enforce employer sanctions in its FY 1999 budget, and the 130 inspectors it requested in the FY 1998 budget proposal were not funded by Congress. *Migration News*, January 1999.

20. Quoted in *Washington Post*, 15 March 1999.

appealing political salve for an extraordinarily difficult set of problems that have no easy short-term solutions.[21] The economist Jagdish Bhagwati has articulated this view with candid clarity. Long before such initiatives as Operations Gatekeeper and Hold-the-Line were conceived, he pointed to India's experience to illustrate the merits of a symbolic show of U.S. force on the border:

> Border enforcement would be sufficiently visible to satisfy those who feel that we should be "doing more" to regain control of our border. In public policy, the advantage of such visible, symbolic action is much too understated. Where a problem is not capable of total solution, such action acquires great importance. Thus, while I believe that the late Prime Minister Indira Gandhi's decision to construct a fence along the enormous India-Bangladesh border in the State of Assam was an ineffective policy . . . I believe that it was nevertheless a splendid policy. For, to be seen to be doing nothing at all, even though one could not really close the border, would have been politically explosive since it would have been read as indifference or indecisiveness. And building the fence was the least disruptive way of doing nothing while appearing to be doing something! [22]

From this perspective, stupid policies can be smart politics. My narrative of policing the U.S.-Mexico border is to a significant extent a story about the political success of flawed and failing policies. Yet as I have also stressed, the enforcement buildup has done far more than simply project an appearance of "doing something," for the collateral damage has been substantial. In the case of U.S. immigration control the death toll along the border continues to rise as migrants are pushed to attempt entry in more difficult and hazardous terrain away from urban areas.[23] In some border areas, the INS crackdown is generating complaints from local residents that their communities increasingly feel like occupied territories.[24] Enforcement pressure also makes migrants more reliant upon a criminal underworld of organized smuggling. Far from seriously deterring illegal

21. Machiavelli, observing that "men in general make judgements more by appearances than by reality, for sight alone belongs to everyone, but understanding to few," advised rulers to "keep the people preoccupied with festivals and shows": quoted in David Kertzer, *Ritual, Politics, and Power* (New Haven: Yale University Press, 1988), 181.

22. Jagdish N. Bhagwati, "U.S. Immigration Policy: What Next?" in *Essays on Legal and Illegal Immigration,* ed. Susan Pozo (Kalamazoo, Mich.: W. E. Upjohn Institute for Employment Research, 1986), 124.

23. Karl Eschbach et al., "Death at the Border," *International Migration Review* 33, no. 2 (1999): 430–54. According to Mexican government statistics, 717 illegal Mexican migrants have died since 1995 in attempts to cross the border. *New York Times,* 18 January 2000.

24. "It's like we've given up our rights because we live by the border," says one California resident. In South Texas, the stopping and searching of vehicles by the Border Patrol has

immigration, then, the border enforcement offensive has instead turned migrant smuggling into a more expansive, corrupting, and profitable business. And this, not surprisingly, has provided a policy justification to increasingly treat illegal immigration as an organized crime problem. Organized crime, in turn, has been officially defined as a growing national security threat.[25]

The escalation of drug control has propelled a partial militarization of the border, with troubling implications. Escalation has also overwhelmed and distorted the criminal justice systems on both sides of the border. And it should not be forgotten that an earlier phase of escalation is what created such a sizable drug-smuggling business along the border in the first place: squeezing the Colombian cocaine pipeline in the Southeast rerouted it to the Southwest, dramatically elevating Mexico's role in the illicit trade. The crackdown on Colombia's traffickers failed to reduce the drug supply but has succeeded in expanding the power and wealth of Mexico's traffickers. It thus fueled greater border corruption and violence, deepened the integration between legal and illegal cross-border commerce, and made the drug problem a more politically explosive issue in bilateral relations.

Border Militarization?

It might be tempting to conclude that the escalatory dynamics along the U.S.-Mexico border must inevitably lead to a progressively more militarized form of control. Indeed, anti-drug operations on the Mexican side of the borderline are already largely in the hands of the military. And this, in turn, may provide further political ammunition and legitimacy for those who advocate a greater military role on the U.S. side. So far, administration officials and key congressional voices have been able to fend off calls for further militarization—partly by promising and promoting more law enforcement.

Proposals to send in the troops are especially popular during election season, when the border often becomes a political stage. For example, during the 1996 presidential race, Bob Dole pledged to expand the National Guard's drug interdiction role and promised that, if such measures

---

become so common that a favorite local joke asks: "Why were you stopped?" The answer: "Driving while Mexican." The Border Control campaign has recently drawn criticism from the United Nations High Commissioner for Human Rights. See Associated Press, 28 November 1999, 3 December 1999; and *New York Times,* 26 January 2000.

25. See Peter Andreas, "The Rise of the American Crimefare State," *World Policy Journal* 14 (fall 1997): 37–46.

proved inadequate, he would turn to the military. Republican presidential candidate Lamar Alexander even proposed creating a fifth branch of the armed forces that would focus on border control tasks.

Some military voices too have advocated expanded law enforcement duties for the troops. In 1991 one former army officer suggested that with the military looking for new work in the post–Cold War era, an "easily accomplished mission for existing forces would be patrolling the borders. It is, of course, absurd that the most powerful nation on earth cannot prevent a swarming land invasion by unarmed Mexican peasants. The U.S. Army is entirely capable of plugging the holes permanently, and border duty would be excellent military training."[26] More recently, writing in the military journal *Parameters,* Major Ralph Peters has argued that the "domestic employment of the military appears an inevitable part of our own future, at least on our borders and in some urban environments. . . . [We are living in a] terribly changed and rapidly changing world" where illegal immigrants, terrorists, drug lords, and organized crime are among the most serious threats. "The U.S. armed forces," he urges, "must change with that world, and must change in ways that are fundamental."[27]

Some prominent security analysts have even advised that the United States should prepare for full-scale military action not only along but across the border in the not too distant future. In *The Next War,* former Secretary of Defense Caspar Weinberger describes key potential future conflicts that U.S. national security strategists should be ready for. In the war scenario closest to home, 60,000 U.S. troops are deployed to the southwestern border after a radical nationalist leader has taken power in Mexico with the help of powerful drug-trafficking interests, and the resulting chaotic situation in Mexico has turned the northward flow of people and drugs into a flood. Unable to plug the border holes, Washington launches a full-scale military invasion. Some six months later, law and order have been restored south of the border. The State Department's postwar strategic assessment of the conflict criticizes the failure of U.S. intelligence to foresee the crisis but praises the military's readiness to intervene.[28] Fortunately, U.S. and Mexican political leaders—as well as Mex-

26. Christopher Bassford, "What Role for the Military Now?" *Newsday,* 17 September 1991.

27. "It is painful to write this. . . . Selfishly, I do not want my Army to change, and my secret fantasies run more to Sherman at Shiloh than to tracking desperate, malnourished economic refugees. . . . It is a miserable prospect to be an officer faced with the need to argue in favor of filthy missions that will never entirely succeed and which will lend endless ammunition to those who loathe the institution that has given worth to my life. I wish it could be otherwise": Ralph Peters, "After the Revolution," *Parameters* 25 (summer 1995): 11–14.

28. Caspar Weinberger and Peter Schweizer, *The Next War* (Washington, D.C.: Regnery, 1996).

ico's drug-trafficking organizations—share an interest in keeping this scenario in the realm of fiction.

Full militarization of the border is inhibited by official opinion in several quarters. Importantly, a much more expansive U.S. military role is strongly opposed by the law enforcement community. While certainly welcoming various forms of military assistance in a support role, enforcement bureaucracies such as the Border Patrol jealously guard their turf. A significantly greater border role for the military is also widely opposed by mainstream political elites and by much of the military establishment itself. Indeed, after a teenage goatherder was fatally shot by U.S. soldiers on a patrol mission along the Texas border in May 1997, the Pentagon indefinitely suspended such operations and indicated an interest in scaling back some of its border duties.

At the diplomatic level, a more extensive and visible U.S. military presence on the border would have poisonous consequences for cross-border ties—both in Washington–Mexico City relations and in relations between local communities along the border. Full-scale militarization would have a disastrous impact on human rights and could significantly impede the booming cross-border commerce that both countries have so enthusiastically encouraged. Sealing the border by military means may be technically feasible (remember the Iron Curtain) but is incompatible with maintaining an open democratic society and sustaining the nation's second largest trading relationship. It would also be highly destabilizing for Mexico, helping to create the very crisis situations that U.S. national security planners hope to avoid.

Despite the Fortress America dreams of some conservative isolationists, the enormous investment that the United States and Mexico have made in the economic integration process necessitates that the border remain highly porous—even while being intensively policed. Tightening controls over the cross-border flow of drugs and migrants while loosening controls over the flow of virtually everything else will no doubt continue to be a formula for policy frustration. How this frustration is politically managed will significantly shape the future of the border region and the bilateral relationship.

BORDERS REMADE

The sweeping global transformations of recent years have prompted widespread declarations about the declining importance of territorial exclusion. Echoing a common view, the geographer Lawrence Herzog claims that the internationalization of the world economy "has led to an inevitable reshaping of boundary functions. The most obvious change has been the shift from boundaries that are heavily protected and militarized to those that are more porous, permitting cross-border social and economic interaction."[29] Students of international relations similarly argue that globalization is about the "unbundling" of territoriality and the "de-bordering" of the state.[30] Even in the realm of immigration, we are told, there is a progressive "desacralization of territory" going on, in which the purposes of the state "become inclusive rather than exclusive or enclosed."[31]

I have pointed to a very different dynamic: one in which borders are transformed rather than transcended, reconfigured rather than retired. In the United States and Western Europe this has involved not only the physical reassertion of border controls but also an ideological redefinition of border functions—reflected in the new prominence of law enforcement in the policy discourse about borders. Here the military defense and economic regulatory functions of border controls may be declining, but their policing functions are expanding. Prohibited cross-border flows are increasingly perceived as threatening to the autonomy, social cohesion, and sometimes even the identity of national political communities. And it is the policing apparatus of the state that is expected and empowered to maintain the boundaries between insiders and outsiders, to enforce law and order, and to project at least the appearance of securing national borders.

---

29. Lawrence A. Herzog, "Changing Boundaries in the Americas: An Overview," in *Changing Boundaries in the Americas,* ed. Lawrence A. Herzog (La Jolla: Center for U.S.-Mexican Studies, University of California at San Diego, 1992), 5–6.

30. John Gerard Ruggie, "Territory and Beyond: Problematizing Modernity in International Relations," *International Organization* 47, no. 1 (1993): 139–74; Lothar Brock and Mathias Albert, "De-bordering the State: New Spaces in International Relations" (paper prepared for annual meeting of the American Political Science Association, Chicago, 31 August–3 September 1995).

31. David Jacobson, *Rights across Borders* (Baltimore: Johns Hopkins University Press, 1996), 41.

Index

Cornell Studies in Political Economy

A SERIES EDITED BY PETER J. KATZENSTEIN

Union of Parts: Labor Politics in Postwar Germany
    By Kathleen Thelen
Democracy at Work: Changing World Markets and the Future of Labor Unions
    By Lowell Turner
Fighting for Partnership: Labor and Politics in Unified Germany
    By Lowell Turner
Troubled Industries: Confronting Economic Change in Japan
    By Robert M. Uriu
National Styles of Regulation: Environmental Policy in Great Britain and the United States
    By David Vogel
Freer Markets, More Rules: Regulatory Reform in Advanced Industrial Countries
    By Steven K. Vogel
The Political Economy of Policy Coordination: International Adjustment since 1945
    By Michael C. Webb
The Myth of the Powerless State
    By Linda Weiss
The Developmental State
    Edited by Meredith Woo-Cumings
International Cooperation: Building Regimes for Natural Resources and the Environment
    By Oran R. Young
International Governance: Protecting the Environment in a Stateless Society
    By Oran R. Young
Polar Politics: Creating International Environmental Regimes
    Edited by Oran R. Young and Gail Osherenko
Governments, Markets, and Growth: Financial Systems and the Politics of Industrial Change
    By John Zysman
American Industry in International Competition: Government Policies and Corporate Strategies
    Edited by John Zysman and Laura Tyson